# DEDICATION

*After the Loss of a Spouse: What's Next* is dedicated to all the widows and widowers who have gone before me. By hearing their stories, I am comforted and inspired. They have experienced the fullness of marriage, the heartbreak of loss, and have found their way to experience life in a new way.

# After the Loss of a Spouse
# What's Next?

Dr. Joanne Zrenda Moore

# Contents

# ACKNOWLEDGMENTS

Many thanks to all those who supported me as I wrote this book. First, my sons, Ned and Steve, and their wives, Lanna and Kristen, who encouraged me as I began the project. Their support was empowering. I appreciate the input from the writers on staff at *Pathfinder: A Companion Guide for the Widow/er's Journey.* Thank you to Lisa Saunders for her chapters on pets and gambling, and to Jane Milardo, LMFT, for her chapter on alcohol abuse. Thank you to the widows and widowers who are walking the path ahead of me, and who have generously shared their stories and advice. Thanks to Michele Delima for her editing. And, of course, I appreciate the memories of my marriage which are a good foundation upon which I will build the next stage of my life.

.

# INTRODUCTION

I was 57 when my husband, Joe, died. Thankfully, I received a good deal of support in terms of grief management—friends, family and work colleagues were truly present for me, and I credit them with my good mental health today. However, none of my friends had yet experienced such an ordeal. Even my parents were still married, so I didn't have a meaningful role model for living as a widow and there were few written resources available to guide me (believe me, I looked everywhere). As I was still quite young and healthy, I knew I should plan for a long life and that it was impractical to sit and wait for my turn to die. And though very sad and disappointed our dreams would not be coming true, I was smart enough to be thankful for the 37 years Joe and I did have together.

Then came a day, about a year after Joe's death, when I discovered (with some surprise!), a bounce in my step. This was a far cry from my slow, grief-induced shuffling gait. My new surge of physical energy…I believe it was my emotional and spiritual energy rising back to their normal levels…prompted me to ask if I was ready to start thinking about my next steps.

I also realized that, despite my lethargy of the past year, I had learned to navigate many aspects of my new life and had accomplished a good deal. But it wasn't easy. I felt like I had to figure everything out for myself. And even when there wasn't an immediate problem, there was always an underlying tone of questioning hyper-vigilance. For instance, I was hearing house sounds I'd never noticed before Did the refrigerator always make that noise? When was the last time the septic tank was pumped? What if there's a storm and the power goes out? What if I get sick? These vague anxieties were constantly present because I didn't have full confidence in my ability to manage everyday problems. I even felt a little angry that no

1

one told me everything I'd need to know to manage a life on my own.

When I was doing my physical therapy training, I was told the best way to learn something is to first watch it, do it, and then teach it. Since it seemed silly to me that each of us in this predicament should have to figure out everything on our own, I decided to write a book to make it a little easier for the next person to transition after the loss of their spouse. It would keep me on my toes and help others. I was excited to have found my next step!

Once I decided to write, I took two weeks off from work and headed up to the Trapp Family Lodge in Stowe, VT. It was January, a great time to devote to such a project. Eager to begin, I pulled the table up to the large window in my room. Gazing out at the easterly view of the snow-covered Green Mountains, I felt such joy watching the sunrise while sipping my steaming cup of coffee. Nestled in here, the writing flowed easily, almost like an energy force. All that I'd bottled up inside came pouring out and I could barely type fast enough.

After a while, I went out for a walk to get some fresh wintry air. I wore grips on my boots to keep me safe on the ice and walked with confidence for four miles. Then, returning to my car, I removed the grips so they wouldn't cause my foot to slide on the gas or brake pedal. Though it made sense at the time, I was so wrong! I slipped right next to my car, breaking my right forearm. Of course I initially denied the injury and continued typing with an iced arm, but it wasn't long before I presented myself to the medical clinic, where an X-ray confirmed my fears and I was casted.

Now remember, I had dedicated this time to writing and the words were flowing. My predicament frustrated me beyond all reason! Not to be deterred (I can be very stubborn), I propped the keyboard up with pillows so it was standing on its side and typed with both hands as if I were playing a clarinet. There was no stopping this book!

During the 12 weeks my wrist was immobilized, I learned to modify my activities so I could still do everything independently, even if done more slowly. And though my initial intent was to lend a helping hand to other widows/ers with my book, along the way, I also found the slower writing pace to be very therapeutic. It gave me time to develop clarity about the structure of my life. And, chapter by chapter, by breaking down the structure into smaller parts, my life became more manageable. Those vague, pesky anxieties were quashed, and I felt my energy and happiness grow.

If you are reading this book, it's likely that you've lost your spouse or partner. Please accept my condolences. It's been six years for me and I'll never forget how Joe's passing pulled the rug out from under me, nor the many days when life felt like a jigsaw puzzle with a bunch pieces missing. And though our situations aren't alike, I feel we share an instinctive bond of compassion, understanding and mutual concern.

Throughout this book, the terms marriage and spouse are used to describe any committed relationship. For each of us, marriage was a significant part of our lives. It provided structure to our everyday activities, and a place in our family and society. Perhaps you had a partner who shared the workload around the house and who was a trusted confidant, or with whom you could laugh and conjure up old memories. Maybe you enjoyed financial security in your marriage or a shared dream for the future. Or perhaps your marriage was one of the many that was difficult - there may have been discord, abuse or other negative aspects. Even then, there's grieving mixed with many other emotions and a major re-adjustment after the loss.

Resiliency, according to the Merriam-Webster Dictionary, is defined as the capacity to return to the original state after a shock or deformation. I'm not sure that resiliency is what we're seeking or what's best for us, however. The marriage and its end did impact us to the extent we will never, and maybe shouldn't ever, return to our original self. We learned a lot during and after the marriage, but it's essential to recognize that changes are occurring, and our perspectives and expectations have evolved.

Yet, in addition to dealing with the grief and disappointment of losing your spouse, you may be struggling in your role as a widow or widower. Maybe a good deal of your struggle with this stage of life - moving past grief and into your new "normal" - happens because you keep trying to be your old self, trying to do things the same way, keep the same activities, and maintain the same social connections. Does the question, "What next?" keep running through your head? Does yearning for security keep you trying to hold on to your old self? Some people feel like they're sitting in God's waiting room with their hands folded, waiting for their turn to die. Others continue doing the same things in the same way, believing that's the way to respect the memory of their loved one. Those two strategies are frequently chosen because they're comfortable, or maybe that's the way an admired grandparent lived out this stage.

However, our generation is different in many ways from those who've gone before. We've had fewer children than previous generations and we tend not to live among a large extended family, upon whom we could rely for company and help. Though we're not especially wealthy, Social Security and Medicare do provide some support after we turn 66. We tend to be more educated than our grandparents, and women, especially, have had career experiences our grandmothers likely never had. The internet has opened new worlds to us. We'll also have more years to live as a widow/er compared to prior generations because our life span has increased.

For this last reason alone it's crucial you accept your altered life! You have years before you to explore countless, wonderful new opportunities, discover and hone your talents, share your love and friendship, and give back to the world. As we know all too well, life is precious and much too short. It's not to be missed. And while it's right to honor your spouse and your marriage, if you're reading this book, understand that's a healthy sign you're ready to begin reassessing your life, seeing what still works and figuring out where you'd be wise to try something new.

Some of the work we need to do is internal, to see ourselves in a new way. But some is also external. We are a part of a community and we need to re-establish ourselves as individuals rather than as half of a couple. Maybe you derived status from your spouse and miss being married to someone "important." If you were in a less healthy marriage, you may find your stock going up by being alone. Maybe your partner was an extroverted social director and now you have to find your own way in the world. Conversely, your partner may've been a home-body and now you're freer to wander.

*After the Loss of a Spouse: What's Next?*, helps you with both the internal and external work to make the most of your life now and in the years ahead. Whatever your age, step by step, it moves you through important topics like deciding where to live, maintaining your health and setting goals. What sets this book apart from others is that it provides strategies you can tap any time to organize your thoughts and actions so you can develop your own rewarding, peaceful life and philosophy.

The exercises in this book help you rebuild your life with small, manageable tasks, relying on the same questioning process I used. You'll certainly come up with your own answers to the questions, and as your philosophy develops, it will be uniquely yours. Having your own philosophy will support you as you strive for the life you want. Without a philosophy, you wander aimlessly, either wasting time or falling into someone else's plan. With a philosophy, you wake every morning with a purpose for the day, the weeks, months and even the years ahead.

There's no need to rush, though. Read a chapter a day or a chapter a week. Start in the middle if you wish and pick what attracts you most. Summon up your curiosity, and grab a pen for taking notes and completing the exercises. There's no right or wrong way to proceed.

You may wish to invite a "buddy" to share the journey with you. It's nice to have someone to brainstorm with, to encourage one another, and to hold one another accountable. This book is also great to use in a group setting - questions within the chapters are great conversation starters! Look to your Hospice support group, church, or even your neighborhood to gather likeminded souls.

I'm so excited to be taking this journey of exploration with you.

To my core, I believe every stage of life has value, including widow/er-hood, and we have the right and responsibility to live it to the best of our ability. It breaks my heart to see people spend precious years disconnected from life after the loss of their spouse. I am not being disrespectful of the grieving process (I still feel waves of grief from time to time). It's important to grieve, remember the wonderful aspects of our marriage, and feel the disappointment that it's over. But think about it this way - would you want someone you love to live with sadness and lack of purpose? Of course not. So why allow yourself to live in that dark place?

We are called to be where our talents meet the world's needs, today and always.

When you're ready to move a step forward to this idea (and I believe you are), take a deep breath and know this book will empower you to forge ahead in a safe, practical, and organized way.

*After the Loss of a Spouse: What's Next?* is about how to live this stage of your life intentionally, be open to meaningful new possibilities, and celebrate your choices. To embrace your changing, evolving self with courage and, yes, even joy.

Ready? Let's begin.

**Before You Get Started**

To help you make this journey as effective and energizing as possible, please keep the following guidelines in mind:

- Remember, there's a big difference between reading and acting on information you learn about. If you're determined to make a positive change in your life, be sure to answer the questions and complete the exercises you find in the chapters ahead.

- Scheduling time to complete each chapter is also a great way to ensure your commitment and success!

- Purchase a special journal and keep it with this book. That way you can immediately answer questions as they come up without searching for paper. Note the date and chapter when you're journaling too; this way, you'll be able to refer back to your work for inspiration and direction—and to see how far you've come on your journey!

- Also keep a dedicated binder or folder handy so you have a safe, organized place for the assessment charts you'll be completing.

# HONORING THE MEMORY

Without our spouse, there's a terrible void in the world. We miss their enthusiasm and the passion they brought to their interests. We feel sorry they didn't get the chance to finish a favorite project.

A wonderful way to prolong the influence of our late spouse's life is to carry on with his or her unfinished work. Some people do this on a grand scale. For example, it's common for a senator's wife to be elected to fill his position, and even heads of state transfer power that way. Most of us don't have such public positions, but we can still act along that line. We simply need to understand our spouse's passion and get involved on some level.

In the beginning, their passions may have included some responsibilities. We become acutely aware of their personal commitments. They may have left responsibilities for his or her parents or children from a previous marriage. You will have to decide how much you can step in and help out. If any of them have special needs, you may choose to help them transition to new caregivers if you're not able to be the caregiver. If any of them were financially dependent, you'll have to work with your new budget to see how much you can continue helping. Being open and honest with your capacity will help them adjust to the changes. Don't make promises you can't keep. Just keeping in touch and continuing to care is important. They, too, have suffered a loss. Sticking together can be very comforting. You have shared experiences to help keep the memory alive, and you may find the continued friendship to be helpful.

Once the everyday responsibilities have been managed, it might be fun to explore other ways to honor their memory. As I searched, I found, on the *Widows Blog*[1], a story about a woman who spent her wedding anniversary

[1] http://modernwidowsclub.com/

day performing random acts of kindness. She purchased gift cards for the cars behind her in the Starbuck's drive through. She placed a bouquet of flowers on the windshield of an elderly couple, and another bouquet on an old gravestone in the cemetery. She placed cash inside a Stephen King book in a bookstore. (Stephen King was her late husband's favorite author). Each token was labeled, A Random Act of Kindness by a Stranger. This young widow then enjoyed dinner (and dessert) with a good friend. Her day was more than a memorial. It was a celebration of her marriage, and she shared the joy of her marriage with others.

Mary MacNeil loves holidays so much that her large family calls her "Holiday Mary." Her late husband was equally enthusiastic and dressed as a very credible Santa each Christmas Eve. After his passing, there was a real void, so Mary dresses up as Mrs. Claus and listens carefully to her grandchildren's wishes.[2]

Ruth Crocker was a newlywed and only 20 years old when her husband was killed in action in Viet Nam. She wrote a book, "Those Who Remain," describing her climb up Eiger Mountain in Switzerland, where they had enjoyed time together, to scatter his ashes. Though now remarried, she still serves on the board of Gold Star Wives of America, an organization serving widows and widowers who have lost a spouse in combat or due to service related injuries.[3]

Eva Franchi lost the love her life in 1990, when her husband Sergio died. He was a world renowned opera star. "Before the three tenors, there was Sergio Franchi," says Eva, "the people's tenor. People loved Sergio." She founded the Sergio Franchi Music Foundation to honor and celebrate his life and music. She opens their estate in Stonington, CT, for a concert every August. Proceeds from ticket sales go to the foundation that awards an estimated 16 grants and scholarships each year to young tenors and sopranos who perform during the concert. To date, 840 grants and scholarships have been awarded to young talent who go on to perform at places like the Metropolitan Opera House in New York, and in Paris, London and Spain. "Who would have known that one day," continued Eva, "this would become the grounds, the stepping stone for today's young upcoming artists, singers, tenors and sopranos honoring the magical world of romantic classical music."[4]

---

[2] Chaffee, PA. Mrs. Claus Creates Memories for Family. *Pathfinder: A Companion Guide for the Widow/er's Journey.* Vol 1 No. 5:14-17.

[3] Chaffee,PA. Ruth Crocker Digs Deep to Tell Her Story. *Pathfinder: A Companion Guide for the Widow/er's Journey.* Vol 1 No. 10:12-15.

[4] Chaffee, PA. Sergio Franchi Memorial Concert. *Pathfinder: A Companion Guide*

My late husband, Joe, came from a farm family in North Carolina. Over the years, the family farm changed hands, and he did not own any part of it. But his childhood memories of summers on the farm shaped his ideas of how life should be. Whenever we went hiking, he'd say his only regret in life was that he did not own any land. Before he became ill, we started taking trips to look for land. After searching for three years, and about two months before he died, we signed the mortgage on 257 acres of young forest in New England. The down payment came from an inheritance from his mother, who'd worked as a nurse all her life and lived very frugally. We felt awkward spending her money on anything frivolous. She was a firm believer in paying off your mortgage as quickly as possible. So that money had sat, waiting for a worthy cause. Joe's intention for the land was to cut lumber every 30 years, so each generation of his descendants would have some help with their mortgage. He also liked the idea of having land because it offered options for lifestyle. Perhaps someday, someone would want to live on the land and farm it. I love the outdoors, and was quite happy with the purchase.

Since Joe's death, I've joined groups that provide education about forestry, attended seminars, and read books about trees. I rely heavily on a forester for advice. All I really do is walk the land, looking for invasive plants and insects. I watch the trees grow, which they do pretty much by themselves. But it is a joy to feel Joe's spirit in those woods, and I feel good that his desires are being carried out. I also really like that my mother's-in-law influence is being honored as well. As with any extended family project, I anticipate there could be problems in future generations, so I'm developing a management structure to keep the land as intended, or allow it to be sold without causing conflict among our descendants.

My friend Judy's late husband was a playwright. At his request, she finished his plays and is working on having them performed. She took one long play and divided it into two shorter plays. She felt comfortable taking some artistic license, as she understood his intentions. Buoyed by the experience, she returned to college and is now enrolled in graduate school, studying creative writing.

Tom Crist of Calgary won $40 million in the lottery. He and his four children have set up a charitable trust so they can give in memory of his wife. The first recipient will be the Tom Baker Cancer Center, as they cared for her prior to her death from lung cancer in 2012 at the age of 57.

Perhaps your late spouse didn't have a special passion or interest. Maybe

*for the Widow/er's Journey.* Vol 2 No 2:14-17.

he was a negative person or even abusive in your marriage. In truth, it's not uncommon. That doesn't mean that you still don't grieve. There is pain in every loss. So how do you honor that person in a way that is honest and helpful? Think about what might help someone else in a similar marriage; you could provide support to a battered women's shelter or soup kitchen. That way you elevate your pain to something positive that's very much needed in the world.

There are also lots of small, affordable things you can do, like making a photo album or transferring your old family films to DVD. You can buy a paving stone at their high school or a town memorial park and have their name engraved on it. You could adopt a child through the Christian Children's Fund and send monthly payments or donate books on a topic she loved to the public library. Plant a tree. Give a scholarship at her high school or college. Give his tools to a young worker just starting out.

**Think of one specific thing that you can do that would carry on the work or the passion of your late spouse.**

It's really nice to have a concrete task that represents our respect for the memory. The finiteness of the task allows us, when it's done, to feel a sense of completion. But even beyond a tangible act, it might be our best tribute to live in a way that would make him or her proud of us. I know that when Joe was alive, he was happiest when I was happy. So, to honor him, I try to find joy in every day.

*Work is love made visible.*

Kahlil Gibran

# ASSESSMENT OF CURRENT LIFE

**In marriage, one compromises each day. Compromise is important in making a marriage work. Now, for the first time in your adult life perhaps, you don't have to compromise! You can do whatever you want! But maybe you haven't thought about it in so long, you don't even know anymore what you want! But you only get one life, so make the most of it.**

It's important to recognize and celebrate those aspects of life that work. These are the parts that bring order and meaning to our days, help us to sleep at night, and fill our hearts with joy. Then, there are those things that fill our days but don't necessarily bring us joy. Lastly, there are things that we do with resentment.

It is one thing to "keep busy," but that is not enough. Your time is a very important commodity. Looking objectively at how you spend your time tells you where your priorities are. You want to take care that you are spending it in ways that enrich your life. Most of us have to stop and think about this awhile.

Most of us have spent our lives doing what needs to be done. We've gotten up early, worked hard to make ends meet somehow, and made check-marks on the to-do lists until our pencils were all used up. The idea of choosing a pastime or a passion was a luxury we didn't linger with. For some of us, our responsibilities are behind us.

But some of us are still responsible for children or family members with special needs. So it is easier for some of us to find discretionary time than for others. But even if you have honest and important responsibilities, try to carve out the time and space for reflection.

For example, author Amy Barry advises parents of young children to define a space in a room, where the children have a quiet art/book activity while the parent also pursues a quiet activity in the same room. [56]

## Part I— Time Analysis Worksheet

To start your assessment of your current life, note your daily activities and mood or attitude during each activity on the following chart. Make copies of chart and complete it hour by hour each day for at least a week. Score each item on a scale of 1 to 10, with 10 being most joyful and 1 being least joyful.

| | Activity | Reason | Joy Scale(1-10) |
|---|---|---|---|
| Midnight | | | |
| 1:00 am | | | |
| 2:00 am | | | |
| 3:00 am | | | |
| 4:00 am | | | |
| 5:00 am | | | |
| 6:00 am | | | |
| 7:00 am | | | |
| 8:00 am | | | |
| 9:00 am | | | |
| 10:00 am | | | |
| 11:00 am | | | |
| noon | | | |
| 1:00 pm | | | |
| 2:00 pm | | | |
| 3:00 pm | | | |
| 4:00 pm | | | |
| 5:00 pm | | | |
| 6:00 pm | | | |
| 7:00 pm | | | |
| 8:00 pm | | | |
| 9:00 pm | | | |
| 10:00 pm | | | |
| 11:00 pm | | | |

[5] Barry, Amy. Caring for Yourself while Caring for Kids. *Pathfinder: A companion Guide for the Widow/er's Journey.* Vol 1 No 8:19-21.

## Part II— Activity Analysis Worksheet

Once you've charted your current life assessment for at least a week—to capture your typical and not so typical days—take a look at the bigger picture. Do your activities fall into categories? How much time do you spend on these activities? Do they bring you joy or pain or something in between?

Use this Activity Assessment to help you get a clear picture of how you spend your waking hours and whether that makes you happy.

| Social Connections | Time per week | Choice or Necessity? | Joy Scale 0-10 |
|---|---|---|---|
| Faith community | | | |
| Neighborhood | | | |
| Clubs | | | |
| | | | |
| Friends | | | |
| Family | | | |
| Dating | | | |
| Social media | | | |
| | | | |
| **Activities** | | | |
| Volunteering | | | |
| Exercise | | | |
| Work | | | |
| Travel | | | |
| Hobbies | | | |
| | | | |
| **Responsibilities** | | | |
| Caring for family members | | | |
| Pets | | | |
| | | | |
| **Budget** | | | |
| | | | |

**What I'd do if I had...**

With that in mind, look carefully at how you spend your time. Eliminate the things that aren't working for you, so that you can have time for the things that are meaningful. As you discard activities or responsibilities, try to be as responsible as possible. For example, if you've always shoveled your neighbor's walk of snow and now you want to stop, be sure to tell your neighbor that you'll no longer be able, and try to give her a name of someone who can take over the job.

It may feel funny at first to have unscheduled time. Learn to be comfortable with inactivity, at least until you decide what to do next.

One of the big problems we widow/ers have is that we have so much love and energy inside us. It's kept bottled up and makes us feel restless and unfulfilled. Let's find a healthy way to use that love and energy, and share it with others and for other causes. (I use the word love here broadly, not necessarily referring to romantic love!)

*Guard well your spare moments. They are like uncut diamonds. Discard them and their value will never be known. Improve them and they will become the brightest gems in a useful life."*

Ralph Waldo Emerson

# PROCESS FOR DECISION MAKING

*"Not to decide is to decide"*

We make decisions all the time. Frozen yogurt or ice cream, a book or a movie, time with friends or time with family, work out or veg out. Most of the time, we fall back on habits without thinking much about it. And we're rarely surprised by an unexpected turn of events.

Food is a great metaphor for all our decision making. One of my nutrition consultants at Thin's In, Diane Rubin, had a poster in the front of her room that said, "If you want different, you have to do different." She was saying that we had to make different food choices if we wanted to lose weight. But she also knew that we had our reasons for eating the way we did. Our families and cultures expected certain things in the cupboards and on the table. We didn't eat or live in a vacuum, where we had total control over our food environment.

Likewise, when it comes to making decisions about our life, we can go on doing the same old thing, whether we like the outcome or not. Or we can take charge and make changes that will help us achieve the outcomes we desire. Again, since we don't live in a vacuum, when we make a change, it affects the people around us. We need to consider our loved ones in our decision making, help them understand our new goals, and include them as much as possible.

Because we put our responsibilities first, we did not feel the freedom to follow our own dreams. But now that we have decided that we want something different, we need to go through a decision making process to help us envision the future in all aspects of our lives.

There are four requirements for the process: defining a vision that serves as our goal, becoming comfortable with risk taking, being comfortable with change, and then assessing our progress.

# DEFINING THE VISION

*Your imagination is your preview of life's coming attractions.*

Albert Einstein

Using your Time Analysis Worksheet and in the Activity Analysis Worksheet, identify which activities you love and wouldn't think of changing. Then identify the things that you do for no good reason, and from which you get no joy. Lastly, identify the middle of the road activities.

**What I love and wouldn't dream of changing:**

If this is a long list, good for you! I'm thrilled you have joyful time in your routine. You might want to find more time for these activities or seek growth opportunities in those areas. If this is a short list, this is your chance to do some brainstorming to expand your horizons. Finding what you do want might be the most difficult part. You may've spent your whole life doing what everyone else needed you to do. This might be the first time you have considered what you'd like to do! So don't rush through this part.

**Take some time alone and recall when you were feeling happy and creative. What were you doing then?**

**Also, what talents do you have?** Remember the Bible story about the talents. (Matthew 25:25). We have a responsibility to develop our best selves. It's not selfish to spend our time taking classes or practicing a skill. In fact, it is by honing our skills that we can make the greatest contributions to the world. We are happiest when our talents meet the world's need. So it's important to recognize your talents.

Here's where I'll offer support for your dropping time consuming activities that don't bring you joy. Each of us has a different talent, and we each contribute a different part to the jigsaw puzzle of life. When we try to fit ourselves where we don't belong, first of all, it just doesn't work. It takes us tremendous energy trying to be something we're not. Let the right person take over that role. Find the gaping hole where you fit perfectly, that no one else can fill. That's where you belong.

You may not yet recognize all the talents within, so list interesting things that you might want to try! The decisions you make here are not cut in stone; once you have a chance to learn more, you can decide whether or not to continue.

Now close your eyes, take three deep breaths, and allow yourself to envision your future. Imagine that all things are possible. What would you try if you had enough support, enough money, or enough confidence? Develop a vision statement based on your hopes and dreams. You can't have a dream come true unless you first have a dream. This vision statement could address work, personal, or financial areas, and will give structure to your planning.

To help you get started, here's my vision statement: My vision is to live with loving relationships, in an environment that supports me as I learn and grow, so that I can access my best level of creativity and be a positive force in the world.

This is my vision because I am happiest when I'm with the people I love. I love to explore new ideas and activities, even when I'm not good at them. But I want to find the talent that is uniquely mine, so that I can leave the world just a little better than I found it.

Now it's your turn.

My vision statement is:

_____

_____

## RISK TAKING:

It's okay to fail. In fact, if you if don't fail from time to time, you're likely not trying anything hard enough. Everyone who accepts challenges fails sometimes. Watch how babies learn to walk. They fall repeatedly, cheerfully picking themselves up over and over again, before they finally master the skill. Even then, the falls occur occasionally throughout childhood as they play with enthusiasm and wholehearted effort. Do they get hurt? Yes, sometimes.

I'm a physical therapist, and I help people recover from such injuries. But I also see patients who have pain that results from a sedentary lifestyle. So, I have come to realize the simple fact that life has pain from time to time, sometimes from being too aggressive and sometimes from being too passive. Since I don't like pain at all, I try to take intelligent risks. The do-or-don't consideration has two sides: Risk versus Reward. Are the possible rewards desired? Maybe fun is the reward, like doing the polka at my son's wedding or the pride of playing a piece on the piano. Sometimes the rewards are very significant, like selling a painting or getting a great job.

Weigh those potential rewards against the risks. Ask yourself what is the worst thing that could happen if things go wrong? Be specific. Too often, we are paralyzed by the fear of very vague negative outcomes. When the exact negative consequence is defined, a solution often presents itself. For example, my friend Betsy, who was recently widowed, wanted to drive 150 miles to visit relatives for Thanksgiving. Her late husband had always done the driving and she wasn't sure she could find her way. She worried about this trip for weeks. Once she realized that getting lost was her greatest possible consequence of failure, she got help in the form of clear directions from AAA, made sure her cell phone was charged, and she successfully made the trip. If you are willing to accept the consequences of failure, should it occur, then go ahead and take the risk. When you do fail, and I hope that you are adventurous enough to meet failure sometimes (hopefully, rarely) just consult your recovery plan. Brush yourself off and learn what there is to learn from the experience. Again, in my work, I spend a lot of time with people who are recovering from failure. The ones who rebound most quickly are those who are able to define and isolate the problem. A patient who was an airline pilot had to be able to quickly rotate his forearm to manipulate the controls to land the plane. Rather than saying, "I can't work anymore," after he sustained serious arm fractures in a biking accident, he built his own piece of exercise equipment that specifically simulated his yoke. Defining the problem specifically allowed him to develop a strategy. He was able to return to flying.

Another common trait I observe is humor. Being able to see the absurdity in the midst of turmoil lets us laugh. Laughing changes our body, relieves stress, and allows us to be creative and open. Laughing also invites positive people into our circle, and they bring energy. Positive people see failure as a state of learning, not as a disaster. We definitely want a network of those positive people as friends who support us through thick and thin. When I was young, I admired people who looked successful. They were attractive, dressed well, and never seemed to stumble. Now, I've come to admire people with scars, bumps, and bruises, sometimes even in wheelchairs, whose sense of humor has drawn smile wrinkles into their faces. These are the people who have loved, suffered and persevered, and with the help of friends, did the best they could.

## COMFORT WITH CHANGE

There are times when we seek comfort by keeping things just the way they've always been. And many times, things should stay the same, or at least the old ways should be remembered and respected. After all, this is why we have national holidays celebrated with tradition. For example, Thanksgiving is an important holiday, designed to encourage us to count our blessings. It begins with the Macy's Day parade, followed by football on television and in backyard pick-up games, and wraps up with the same turkey centered meal year after year. It is nice to have that holiday toward the end of the year, to look back and appreciate the accomplishments and people in our lives.

But if every day were lived in such a way – that is, if we always knew the exact plan and outcome of the day – then life would be quite dull. And we'd have nothing new to celebrate on the next Thanksgiving. It's good to have a combination of old and new. We need enough "old" for security and comfort, and enough "new" to make life interesting.

Remember to use your Time and Activity Assessment Worksheets to decide where you might make some desired changes. Is it time for you to make some changes that might spice up your life? How about starting with a simple change that is easily reversed if need be? For example, if you re-arrange your living room furniture, you can put it right back if it doesn't feel right. Or if you're a caregiver, get a companion to sit with a dependent family member while you take a painting class. Maybe try a new recipe. Being in a rut is a state of mind, and small changes can really help you start seeing the world differently, and to see the opportunities that are available. Small changes help build your confidence, too; you will start to understand that failure isn't fatal, as you recover from small stumbles.

Remember, no change happens in a vacuum. What you do affects the people around you. Some of your changes will be welcomed by your loved ones. In fact, they may have been suggesting for years that you go on a trip with the seniors or out with new friends. And when you're out independently and having fun, your loved ones can feel "off the hook." They feel freer to wander and live without constant concern for your welfare. On the other hand, if you've been a reliable babysitter for grandchildren, their parents may need to make other arrangements that day. So be aware how your new activities may impact others.

Also, communicate well and respect that you are a member of a community. When your loved ones understand the changes that you're making, they can also provide support. As you gain confidence in trying new things, you'll have an air of joyful energy about you. Some people won't be comfortable with the new you. You'll have to figure out why. Most of the time, it's easy. If you're starting a fitness program, your doughnut buddy might feel left behind. You can still share a cup of coffee and a healthier snack. But if you're an alcoholic and you're going to join AA, then there might be some friendships that will be neglected until they also join.

Just be aware that change is scary, not just for you, but for those around you, too. So start small, build your confidence, and develop a network of people to support you. But most of all, remember that the vision is yours. The amount of risk that you're willing to take on is your decision, and you will only accept a risk if you can manage the consequences of any failure that might ensue. This experience can be fun and interesting and meaningful. You're going to meet great people. And in the end, the change you'll make will bring you joy.

# FINANCES

I was taught to never discuss money. My mother said that there will always be someone with more and someone with less. She was also quick to point out that "class" has nothing to do with wealth. She described class as the art of making everyone around you comfortable.

I'm tempted to end this chapter right here.

Maybe I should.

No, I think we can talk about money in a way that is practical and helpful. After all, it's a currency that fuels our lifestyle. The way we manage the money we have allows us to accomplish our desired goals. I've seen people with a lot of money live meaningless existences, and I've seen people with very little money living well.

Oftentimes, the biggest mistakes we make after the loss of our spouse are financial. And financial advisors say that the first problem develops because the widow/er doesn't have a good handle on income versus expenses. None of us like a budget, but it's an important tool for helping us live within our means. The stakes are high. Getting into debt makes us vulnerable. We may lose our home. We may have to take in boarders who are difficult. We may have to take a second job. For all these reasons, it's important to live a little below our means so that we can save a bit each month for emergencies.

As food is important to me, I'm going to use another food metaphor. When I started my "lifestyle change," my dietician, Rosemary Collins, had me keep a food journal for two weeks. I was not to change any of my usual diet, just simply document my food and drink intake. At the end of the time, we reviewed my journal. We added up the calories and the percentage of fat, protein, and carbohydrates. Then she asked me which of the foods I'd be willing to do without. When those were whittled out, I still had enough to feel satisfied.

This strategy works great to better understand your financial expenditures as well. Using a credit card makes it easy to do this at the end of the month; that combined with a check register to document our bigger expenditures. But keep a notebook for documenting small outlays too. If you have big expenses that you pay once or twice a year, like car insurance, pro-rate the amount so that you can have a monthly figure to enter.

The purpose of this exercise is to see clearly where your money goes so you can understand whether your financial outlays reflect your true value system. When I did this, I realized that I was automatically deducting money each month for two very similar home video options. Just by paying closer attention, I was able to save $10 a month. That might not seem like much, but when I'm able to contribute $120 to my favorite charity, it's a better use of the money. And I'm not doing without anything I need. It's just smart to be aware and cost efficient. Your list will include categories described in this table plus any you need to add:

| Total monthly income | $ | |
|---|---|---|
| Monthly Expenses | Amount | Planned change |
| Rent/mortgage | | |
| Utilities | | |
| Insurance | | |
| Phone | | |
| Internet, cable, social media | | |
| Taxes | | |
| Groceries | | |
| Eating out | | |
| Car payment/public transportation/Gas | | |
| Medical/dental/pharmacy | | |
| Clothing | | |
| Gifts | | |
| Charitable donations | | |
| Entertainment, vacation | | |
| Loan payments | | |
| Pets | | |
| | | |
| Total expenses | | |
| **Net Remaining** | | |

Are you surprised by any of your expenses? Did you spend on something you really don't care about? **Is there anything you'd like to do to free up money for more important things? Think of it this way when you cut an item from your expenses: It's not doing without. It's finding money for things that you really do care about.**

Mostly, become familiar with your monthly cost of living and stay within your means. Not keeping track of monthly income versus expenses is the single most common mistakes made by widow/ers. The most common mistake that widow/ers make is in the realm of money management. It's important to know how much money comes in every month, and how much you are spending.

If you spend more than comes in, you will have trouble. Adjust your expenses to rebalance your cash flow, then explore ways to increase your income so you can maintain or raise your standard of living

Remember, you don't have to duplicate the way you've been living. To develop a new lifestyle, keep the parts that suit you and be creative about how you'll live.

### Lump Sum Insurance

Another mistake is poor management of a lump sum insurance payment. What seems like a lot of money can quickly be gone if it's kept where it is readily available. It should be saved in such a way that it is safe and has potential for growth. Meet with a qualified financial advisor to determine how to manage long term investments. If you need help with developing a monthly budget, ask for that, too. It can be tricky to find a financial advisor who you trust and can afford. Your financial manager should be more interested than interesting.

Ask financial managers how they make their money. Commission-based advisers collect a fee on every transaction. They earn a percentage of those sales from the corporation or company that offers them. This means their choices of investments for you could be more influenced by a third party than by your needs or goals. Fee-based advisers work with you on an hourly basis as a consultant, giving you advice which is up to you to implement. Or they can manage your investments for a management fee, irrespective if your account balance goes up or down. Their motivation is to keep you happy by providing good service so you keep your account with them. And they'd also prefer to see your account balance grow so that they can earn a larger fee. Thus, generally speaking, the interests of a fee-based adviser are aligned with your own.

Let me be very direct about the role of a financial adviser in your life. Your money is your money – not the adviser's money. If you are not comfortable with your adviser for whatever reason, then you should end the relationship and switch to another one. Make sure they listen closely to you, communicate clearly with you, and make you feel like you are being well taken care of.[7]

### Long-term Insurance

If you don't have long term care insurance, I encourage you to look into it. Long term care insurance covers some expenses for you if you're not able to take care of yourself. This policy starts coverage if your doctor feels you need help to live independently or in a care facility. You pay a premium starting now. If you need help, due to injury or disability, the policy will cover a wide variety of services to be delivered in your home or in a facility. Of course, policies vary. Most cover home health care for assistance with personal needs. Some cover equipment like chairs that transport you up the stairs or a chair that helps you stand. Some even help with paying someone to shovel snow or mow the lawn. Read the fine print. If you choose well, it increases your chances of living independently and safely in your own home without being a burden to your children.

On an annual basis, reassess to make sure you are getting the best price for appropriate insurance. Meet with your insurance agent or go online to be sure you're appropriately insured for your car, home and health. An insurance broker deals with many insurance companies and can help you to compare.

---

[7] Somberg, Matthew. *Pathfinder: A Companion Guide for the Widow/er's Journey.* Vol 1. No 1. Financial. www.widowedpathfinder.com

# HOME

Whether your current living situation is humble or grand, you spend a lot of time at home. It should be a refuge from the world, a place where you find peace. It should also be functional and its conveniences should enhance your life. It seems so simple, doesn't it!

Just the word *home* conjures up all sorts of emotional images for me. I tell my kids that whenever, and wherever, we're all together, I'm home. For me, home is where my loved ones are. I still live in the house where I raised my children, where I cared for my mother-in-law after she had a stroke and could no longer live alone, and where my husband died. That house contains all the memories of the past 40 years. I am incredibly attached to the place.

Being a physical therapist influences how my home is set up. It started as a 2 story cape, with 3 bedrooms upstairs. Knowing that I am getting older, but also that I would like to stay independent and safe in my home for as long as possible, I added a first floor bedroom and handicapped accessible bathroom. I use the bedroom as a family room for now, but will transition its use when I don't feel safe on stairs anymore. Putting on the addition took a year from start to finish. I wanted to do the work while there was no urgency, so that I could take my time with all the little decisions that had to be made along the way. It's set up now so that I have a very efficient kitchen, living/dining area, bedroom, and bathroom/laundry. I could easily live in that space only, closing off the rest of the house if necessary. I was feeling pretty good about that. Then, a few storms knocked the power out, and I didn't feel so secure. So I had a generator put in. This is one that is connected directly into the circuit breaker so that I don't have to remember how to safely work a system. It's also propane powered, so I don't need to handle a heavy can of gasoline.

My contractor, Patrick McAneeny, told me that many of his customers are widow/ers. Maybe we renovate our homes as a nesting strategy. So much of our world fell away when our spouse died. We like to have some security in our home

Before putting too much money into a renovation, decide first whether this home is where you want to stay for a long time. This is a really big decision, and worth time to explore. Here are some questions to get you started:

What does home mean to you?

- Is it simply a place to store your stuff and lay your head at night? Is it just a temporary stop along your way?
- Would you like to be near family?
- Is it a financial investment?
- Is it a place where you entertain friends?
- Are friendly neighbors important to you?
- Do you like living in an urban or small town environment?
- Do your family members like to celebrate holidays with you?
- Do you like taking care of a yard or garden?
- Do you need a place for woodworking projects or auto repair?
- Do you need a place for your pet?
- Do you like to drive, or must you live near public transportation?
- If you travel, would you like to be near an airport?
- Do you need to live near a VA hospital or military installation, or maybe near a certain medical center?
- How much space do you need, and how much space are you willing to maintain?
- Do you want to be near recreational facilities like a YMCA or walking trails?
- How much of your budget do you want to spend on housing?

## DECIDING WHERE TO LIVE

Obviously, the first choice is to stay put. That's a valid decision if you love your current home and if it meets your needs in a practical, affordable way. If you decide to stay, look at the house with both your heart and your head, and think about your physical capacity to keep it up and your financial resources. What helps with this analysis is that you have accurate information about what it costs to maintain your house. You also can anticipate future repairs or upgrades that would develop. Updating things like the roof will allow you to do these big projects on your own budget schedule. When routine maintenance is neglected, unexpected and large expenses can develop.

Your second choice is to downsize in the same community. There are fabulous over 55 housing developments everywhere. Most are built in an architectural style called Universal Design, which means that architectural barriers are minimized. Most towns also zone now for affordable housing to be included with any new development. You know the neighboring towns, too, so you can consider a move that meets your housing need without losing close proximity to your friends and family.

If you decide to move, your choices are endless. Many widow/ers need to move away to feel free to start over. They find the memories too painful to stay put. You can really have some fun exploring new neighborhoods, towns, and cities. Money Magazine features America's best towns in various categories. Real estate companies have their listings on line so that it's easy to get virtual tours of homes and neighborhoods. If you see something attractive, taking a vacation to a potential new town might be helpful. Take time to visit the town's recreation facilities, the library, houses of worship, and coffee shops. Clubs like Toastmasters International and volunteer organizations like Habitat for Humanity always welcome visitors. Read the local newspaper, and look for the calendar of events section. Read the Letters to the Editor to understand some of the issues of the town.

Real estate agents are very happy to show you a few listings, and orient you to the personalities of the neighborhoods. Keep a notebook handy and write down your impressions. If you can afford it, try renting in a potential new town for at least 3 months before moving. While you're there, make every effort to connect with new friends and activities. Moving to a new town provides opportunities for all sorts of new growth and adventures that would not be possible any other way.

The most common complaint that I hear about home, regardless of geography, is that it's just too quiet. We miss the sounds of another person about. We can get out of the house for all sorts of reasons, but sooner or later, we come back home. We turn the key in the lock, open the door, hang up our coat, and hear the deafening silence. This is, of course, not as easy to address as geography. And there is no one right solution. Some people find great solace in having a pet. People who have dogs feel a very warm welcome when they come in. But I'm not sure that even a favorite dog completely fills the void. Some people find it's a good idea to get a roommate. When my mother-in-law was widowed, she took college students in to live in her garage apartment. It was nice having someone on the property to chat with occasionally and to help with the heavier tasks. It helps with the budget, too. If you can take in a boarder, that can provide some company too. Just be sure to interview well so the boarder understands your rules. You might want a lawyer to draw up a lease agreement and do a background check on the person.

For me, I like public radio talk shows and some talk shows on TV. I record the shows I like so I can view them as I wish. Sometimes I'll make a phone call, to connect with a cousin or a friend I haven't talked with in a while. I'm sure you've already tried those things. Yet, when the day is done, the house is quiet, and sometimes it's just hard.

That's why, someday, I'd love to find a way to combine community living with the feel of a stand-alone house. Here's my dream: I envision a home with a large community living area and kitchen, maybe a library/computer room, a laundry area, guest bathroom, and craft/hobby area. And off of that large area would be four suites consisting of a small living room, bedroom, and bathroom. Outdoors, off of each suite would be a patio and room for a small garden. There would be a four car garage with storage space for each resident, and shop space for projects. Above the garage could be an apartment for visiting family members. The first four residents would be amicable people who live independently but enjoy the company of others. There are several ways to work the financial arrangements; for example, one person could own the building and rent to three others; four people could purchase equal shares in a partnership with rent sufficient to cover all maintenance costs. There would also be a clear policy and procedure manual for rights and responsibilities of both the landlord and the tenants. It's important, as Steven Covey says, "to start with the end in mind." So there would also need to be a way for people to move out when they choose to live with a romantic partner or a child, or when they can no longer function safely, or when they'd simply like to move on. Partnership agreements and leases should be very clear on this.

Wherever you live, home should be a comfort not a stress. When you come in, if things are right, your muscles relax, your rate of breathing decreases, and you get that cozy feeling inside. It should be easy to find things, to do things, and to sleep well.

To be able to find things, the clutter must be organized. You might start by throwing out stuff or by putting it into storage boxes somewhere accessible, but not necessarily in your daily path. It is fun to go to an office supply store and get file folders, labels, and organizers. That shopping trip will bring memories of the first day of school. There is an excitement to beginning such a project.

To do things, you should have all the little tools required for most tasks. I have one drawer in my kitchen for the tools that I know how to use, in addition to tape, measuring tape and wall hangers. The basement houses the rarely used tools and stuff that I hope my sons will take home with them someday.

And to sleep well, you should have a good bed, a dark room, and, as my late husband would say, a clear conscience. Sleeping well is incredibly important, and we'll talk more about that in the chapter on health.

## FOOD

One thing that makes a house a home is the comforting aroma of our favorite foods cooking in the kitchen. Whether it's a savory spaghetti sauce or a sweet gingerbread, food turns ordinary days into special occasions. Just because we're alone doesn't mean that we are sentenced to eating hard boiled eggs and canned peaches every night. If you have always done the cooking, then you might find it easy to manage meals that are nutritious and delicious. Your problem may be that you have always cooked for a crowd, or maybe you're just tired of cooking. This chapter is for you, as well as for those who have not yet found their way around the kitchen.

How we are eating is a pretty good indicator of our emotional state. I will worry about you if I come in and see empty pizza boxes strewn around, and only some mustard in the refrigerator. I want to see that you have a bowl of fresh fruit, some whole grain breads, some yogurt, and some sort of protein around. Maybe you'll have some green tea or water with lemon slices. Food is an important way that we care for ourselves, and comfort ourselves. Especially during times of stress, our bodies need to be well nourished.

I had the privilege of speaking with world renowned chef, Jacques Pépin, about how we can eat well alone, and on a budget. He graciously confessed that, when alone, even he stands at the stove and eats directly from the pot. But he also gave some helpful hints. Prepare dinner in the grocery store. From the salad bar, select some olives and artichokes, then head over to the deli and ask for a few slices of ham atop, and voila – instant dinner! If you're feeling a little more adventurous, buy a cooked chicken, and pair with your favorite rice and vegetable. Use leftovers for sandwiches, soups, or casseroles. Or pick up some local fresh eggs and build an omelet with some sautéed vegetables.

Consider taking a cooking class. You'll find them at kitchen stores, in adult education programs, and in community settings. Not only will you learn several recipes that you can repeat at home, but you will also meet some people.

Eating well takes some planning. Before you head to the grocery store, write out a menu for the week. Include all 3 meals, plus some healthy snacks. Use the cookbook so you have all the ingredients for your recipes. Meals prepared in a crock pot are easy and will give your house that comfortable aroma. If you're in the mood for cooking something big, invite a friend over to share. Or pick up storage bags or plastic containers so you can freeze leftovers for another time. Another good use of leftovers is to deliver a meal to someone who is going through a difficult time. Your gesture of friendship will be appreciated.

## This might be a good time for tea and a muffin!

### Morning Glory Muffins[8]

**Ingredients**

1-cup canola oil

1-cup raw cane sugar

4 eggs

1/3 tbsp. vanilla extract

1-cup general-purpose flour

2 tsp. cinnamon, 2 tsp. baking powder, 2 tsp. baking soda, ½ tsp. salt

1/8 cup flax seed

½ cup walnuts, ½ cup dried coconut, 1/3-cup raisins

1½ cups of grated carrot

**Method for 6-8 muffins**

Sift the flour and dry ingredients into a bowl. Whisk the eggs, canola oil sugar and vanilla together. Grate the carrots.

Mix the walnuts, coconut and raisins and coat in a little of the dry mixture.

Mix the dry ingredients into the egg mixture. Fold in the nut mixture. Lastly add the grated carrots.

Put the mixture into a non-stick spray coated baking tin or use muffin cases. Bake in a preheated oven at 350 degrees for about 4o minutes.

---

[8] Collins, Rosemary. Recipes from the White Gate Farm. *Pathfinder: A Companion Guide for the Widow/er's Journey.* Vol 2 No 3:30-34.

# IN CASE OF ILLNESS

In case of illness, your home should be a refuge. The medicine cabinet should be stocked with up-to-date medicines including prescription and over-the-counter items. Include anti-diarrhea, anti-histamines, cough medicine, cold medicine, lozenges, allergy medicine and aspirin/ pain relievers. You should have a thermometer and a blood pressure cuff. Your pantry should have chicken noodle soup, Gatorade, and Jell-O. If you're ill, you should let someone know so that they can check on you at least once a day. That person should know your doctor's name and contact information.

If you can't decide whether or not to call 911, call it. Let the professionals decide on a diagnosis and plan of care.

In your wallet, keep a record describing your medical history, medications you take, your blood type, the name of your primary care doctor, the name of the person who has your medical power of attorney, and contact information of who you'd like called in case of emergency. Your health insurance information should also be readily available.

It's a good idea to have a friend willing to drive you to appointments that make driving yourself difficult; for example, if you are to have a procedure that requires anesthesia, you will not be allowed to drive yourself home.

# IN CASE OF STORMS/POWER OUTAGES

Be sure to have your home stocked with things that you'd need "just in case." If your home is to be a safe harbor, it should function if there's a power outage. If there is a storm coming, be sure to stock your pantry with enough food to keep you for a few days. That food should be easy to prepare if the power is out. Meanwhile, try to use up the food in the freezer in case the power goes out.

Keep a "go bag" packed in case you need to evacuate to a shelter. It took me a full week-end to assemble my go bag. You think you know where everything is, until you reach for it! Here's the list:

### Emergency Evacuation Kit
Keep emergency evacuation kit by an exit door in a wheeled duffle bag.
- ☐ Emergency drinking water – one gallon per person per day.
- ☐ 1 Collapsible Water Carrier.
- ☐ Four 2400 Calorie Food Packets
- ☐ Emergency Survival Blanket
- ☐ Four Light Sticks, 12 hours each
- ☐ Flashlight with the correct type of batteries (waterproof is preferred)
- ☐ Two hand warmer packs
- ☐ Emergency poncho for warmth or rain
- ☐ 2 changes of clothing plus pajamas
- ☐ Assorted hygiene
  - ☐ Toothbrush

- ☐ Toothpaste
- ☐ Soap
- ☐ Deodorant
- ☐ Shampoo
- ☐ Lotions
- ☐ Comb
- ☐ Toilet tissue
- ☐ Facial tissue
☐ Assorted first aid
- ☐ Prescription medications, allergy medications, pain relievers
- ☐ Band-Aids
- ☐ Gauze
- ☐ Antibiotic cream
- ☐ Triangular bandage
- ☐ Ace bandage
- ☐ Ice bag
- ☐ Tweezers
- ☐ Scissors
- ☐ Moist toilettes
- ☐ Alcohol prep pads
- ☐ Safety pins
- ☐ First aid booklet
☐ Forty dollars in quarters or small bills
☐ Photo Identification (copy of driver's license)
☐ Copies of certificates/licenses, deed, insurance policies
☐ Crank-powered radio
☐ Contact information of friends and relatives
☐ Fast food restaurant gift certificates
☐ Air filter mask
☐ Latex protective gloves
☐ Small waste bags
☐ Whistle
☐ Telephone and charger
☐ Emergency whistle
☐ Work gloves
☐ Tie down rope
☐ Duct tape
☐ Recreational activities like books, puzzles, cards.
☐ AUTO ACCESSORIES:
- ☐ "Call Police" Banner
- ☐ 2 Rolls Duct Tape (2" x 15')
- ☐ Emergency Flare (45 mins.)

# DISCRETIONARY TIME

We all know that a job expands to fit the time we have. So the concept of free time may be a tricky concept to define. But, hopefully, the Time Activity Analysis helped you realize you do have some discretionary time. Discretionary time is that which is available for your own intentional use. It's free of responsibility and previous commitments. It is your greatest possession. This is where you have potential for the INCREDIBLE to happen. Because of this incredible potential, this time should be defined and protected from intrusion by unimportant distractions.

If there is something you've always wanted to do, this is your chance! Consider yourself lucky if you know yourself well enough to know your passion. All you have to do is create an environment conducive to channeling your energy. Find the teacher, the place, the money, the equipment, the self-discipline. Develop a system of accountability to keep yourself on track.

Most of us have to stop and think about this awhile. Most of us have spent our lives doing what needs to be done. We've gotten up early, worked hard, made ends meet somehow, and made check-marks on the to-do lists until our pencils were all used up. The idea of choosing a pastime or passion was a luxury we didn't linger with, or available only in retirement with responsibilities behind us. Now, with more available discretionary time, this is your opportunity to make your passions and interests come to life.

**How we use our discretionary time is what makes our life intentional. This is the time that develops our talent, contributes to the people or cause we love; that truly makes our unique mark**

**upon the world. It's the important time. When we look back on our lives we'll say, I'm so glad I made time for...**

To help you envision your passion and interests, and preserve discretionary time for *you*, complete the following sentences here or in your journal:

I was most happy when I:

I've always wanted to learn to:

People tell me I'm good at:

There's an organization whose work I admire, and I'd like to lend a hand. That organization:

Someone I'd really like to make peace with is:

Somewhere I've always wanted to go is:

If I had money, I would:

If I had more confidence, I would:

Ways to follow up on these ideas include:

People/organizations who could help me with this include:

What theme or patterns emerge in your answers? Try ranking the top ideas above, then schedule time to do one or two in the upcoming week! And remember, these ideas are not written in stone. This activity that you choose now will serve a purpose. Once that purpose is achieved, you can move onto another chosen activity.

Have you ever been busy, and said to yourself, "When I have time, I need to..." Keep a notebook and write down that idea. Then, when you find yourself with some free time, consult your list. It's your own version of the "honey do" list. The days of wandering aimlessly around the house are over!

# WORK

Work is so much a part of who we are. Whether paid or volunteer, it's a way to be creative and make contributions to our community. I believe that work is important at any age or stage, because it makes us part of a community, and because it gives us purpose. The value of paid work has become increasingly evident over the past decade. High unemployment has set many of us back. So the reality is that most of us have to work to pay the bills.

Some financial advisors recommend that we divide our portfolio between stocks and bonds at a ratio that correlates to our age. For example, if we are 60, then 60% of our money should be in stocks, and 40% in bonds. Perhaps we should divide our work/play time in a similar but inverse manner. When we were young, we worked all the time. Now, maybe we can afford to consider discretionary activities. This system might allow us to contribute our experience and wisdom to ongoing projects, and still have time for new things we'd like to try.

If you have been out of the workforce for a while, whether by choice or because you were laid off, or because you took time out to be a caregiver, you might feel overwhelmed by the changes that have occurred while you were away. In no time in history has so much change happened in so short a time. Even people who have not been out of the work force feel a need to constantly upgrade their skills. You are not alone when you realize that you may need to hone your skills in order to go back to the same job. If you go back to a job similar to your previous work, you'll soon catch up. Just go in with a learner's humility and find a mentor to support you. Or, you might want to pursue a different line of work; this can be your opportunity to try something new if you didn't really love your old work. If so, consider working with a life coach. Life coaches are often social workers or psychologists. They can administer a battery of tests to help you determine what type of work you would do well and enjoy.

Before you go back to work, there are two lists you need to make. One list details what skills, experience and talents you bring to the workplace, and the second helps you understand the best work environment for you. In this manner, you get to know yourself. You probably have more to offer than you realize. Be sure to include:

### Skills, Experience and Talents Assessment

- Personality traits. Be honest, because there is a spot for every type of person. You want to end up where you'll fit in, so there's no point in saying what you think the manager wants to hear. As an employer, I want to know if you are a team player. Will you contribute your ideas and experience? Can you work to support a decision that has been made? Will you persevere? Are you honest? Are you a learner? Are you the person who can find the problems in an organization and help find ways to improve it?

- Volunteer work: Any project counts. If you organized a rummage sale, you can do just about anything. If you were a youth group leader, it tells me you go above and beyond. If you are the person who arrives early to make the coffee before a club meeting, you are someone I can depend on.

- Personal experience: Be careful here to describe your experience, but recognize that your life is unique and may not carry over into the work world. For example, if you cared for a person with an illness, and you're applying to work as a companion, know that each family has a unique way of managing themselves. You'll need to be adaptable.

- Education: Include formal education, even if it's not in the field you're applying for. Also include continuing education courses you've taken, and if you speak a second language. Note the books or journals you read frequently. If you belong to learning groups, like a book club or Toastmasters Club, list that, too.

- Hobbies: Hobbies may tell something about you; for example, quilters attend to details and have great persistence.

- Work capacity: Know yourself well enough to seek a job that you can physically and emotionally handle. For example, how much can you lift and how often? How long can you sit? Do you have patience?

- Special skills: Include computer, art, photography, public speaking to give employers a better idea of what you bring to the table.

- References: Who will give you a personal or professional reference? Any time you leave a position, even if it's volunteer, ask a manager or a colleague for a written letter of reference. Or, ask them if you could use their name as a reference in the future.

Looking at this first list should give you a good level of confidence when you go for a job interview. When you include these things in a resume, it gives the interviewer topics to address. Some of your specific details might create a connection with the interviewer.

Now complete these next questions to better understand the ideal work environment for you:

**Work Environment Assessment**

- What type of work would you find interesting? Do you like an office job, or being out in the field? Do you like administration or hands-on?
- Do you need certain hours or a certain income?
- What sort of supervision do you need?
- What training do you need?
- Do you prefer working autonomously or on a team?
- How do you feel about being a leader?
- Is this just a temporary job, or would you like to see opportunities for growth?
- Do you need benefits like health insurance or paid vacation?
- Are you willing to be an independent contractor? This requires that you supply your own equipment, carry liability insurance, and pay appropriate taxes.

Armed with answers to these questions, you'll be better able to analyze available job listings and apply for appropriate positions. The better you know your needs, the better you can choose something that will be a good fit for yourself and for the employer. Some job listings are available in the newspaper. But more often now, you need to go to sites like Monster.com or a company's website to look for openings. And the applications are made on-line without any opportunity for personal connections. If you need help, ask a librarian how to do a search; public libraries often run free classes on job searches. The state unemployment office should also be a great resource. And don't overlook one of the most effective strategies out there: networking. Let people you volunteer with know that you're open to a paid position. They may know people who might be hiring and can give a personal reference for you.

Taking a job is the fastest way to a paycheck and to social networking. But if you're feeling adventurous, and can afford it, this might be a chance for you to start your own business. It's risky, and you certainly will not collect a quick paycheck, but the start-up phase is very creative and exciting, and you can take your passion to a new level. For instance, I've seen people do well selling cupcakes. On the other hand, I know people who lost everything in failed attempts of big projects like turning a house. Only take risks that you can afford to take if it fails. If starting a small business is a new concept to you, ask for mentoring from such agencies as the Small Business Administration or SCORE. They'll help you write a business plan and get financing. There are great courses at community colleges. How to start a small business is beyond the scope of this book. But if it's what you want to do, you have my admiration and best wishes.

# PARENTING

Being a single parent is difficult under any circumstances. Just the physical energy required to manage the lives of children is tremendous. Then there is the financial responsibility that is yours alone, when most households feel they need two incomes. When you add to that the emotional layer of losing your spouse and your children losing their parent, it is overwhelming. Surely, in our dreams on our wedding day, this was a scenario that never entered our minds. Few of us have a ready role model to follow, so I'll start by saying there is no one right way to manage this situation. Each is unique. Your family history and culture, your relationship with your children, and your late spouse's relationship with the children, the cause of death, your health and that of your children, are all factors that will influence your decision making.

Though you may feel you are alone, please know you are not. A surprising number of people die at young ages. Half a million Americans each year are widowed under the age of 45. If you are open to it, you will begin finding others in the same situation and you can learn with them. The old African adage, "It takes a village to raise a child" is certainly true here. You will find support from wonderful people along the way. Some will be in your geographic community, but on-line groups are also very helpful. On-line groups are available 24/7, so busy parents can participate on their own schedule. There are also retreats like Camp Widow, where people can find others in a similar situation.

Your most important rule to live by is Take Care of Yourself! Just as the flight attendant instructs us to put our own oxygen mask on before helping our neighbor, we are no good to anyone unless we are reasonably okay ourselves. So find a counselor—your hospice group or pastor or family practice doctor should be able to give you a reference—and get your grief work started. Nurture your friendships, and share your feelings and confidences with them, as they can be good sounding boards for you. This will allow you to vent away from the children.

Meanwhile, assure your children that you will be all right, even if you're not right now. They will take their cues from you. Model that grieving is normal and natural, and that being sad is understandable. Crying is not a sign of weakness. It's okay for you to cry and it's okay for them to cry. Even though you are sad, you are still there for them. They can count on you. You cling to the people you have left, and you appreciate one another.

The children will experience other emotions that are also normal—like being scared of losing you and being angry at the situation. They need to know you can handle it if they express these feelings. When you allow them to communicate their feelings, you have a good window into how they are doing. Then, you can support them as they need. It may be true they will have to grow up a little faster and accept more responsibility, but they are still the children and you are still the parent.

Children will grieve over and over again, as they are able to process the loss at each developmental stage. They will ask questions with greater detail as the years go by. They will want to know more about mom or dad, and how they felt about things; they'll want to hear the stories. Share with them what is appropriate for their level of understanding.

You cannot be two parents. You are only yourself. So be the best self that you can be, and have the best relationship with each child that you can. Spend time together on art projects, hiking outdoors, playing games, making music, cooking, or whatever interests you may share. Your time together is your best blessing. Teach that being happy is okay, too. It is okay to laugh, to dream, to play practical jokes. The sadness of the loss is a part of your life that teaches us to appreciate what we still have.

Celebrating Mother's Day or Father's Day, or your spouse's birthday can be a special occasion. It's a great time for storytelling. You can make it a time to honor the parent in some way. For example, if the parent loved to read, make a donation to the public library or give some books to a child care center. Or if they loved music, play some old albums or go to a concert. It might be a time to visit your in-laws or some old mutual friends.

Encourage your children to develop friendships. They need peers, too, to bounce ideas off of and to have "kid" fun. Allow them to leave you for an overnight or for camp. You will find it helps them grow in confidence and gives you some quiet time.

There are a few other things to consider. Your children have concerns about losing you, too. And though unlikely, it is possible. So when you see your lawyer, make sure your will designates who will parent your children in case of your death. Let your children know that this plan is in place. If possible, take out a life insurance policy that will cover the expenses for the custodial parents.

Eventually, you may choose to remarry. Some children may find relief from responsibilities when another adult joins in. Others are thrilled to have a new "mom" or "dad." It's also possible there could be jealousy over the relationship, so introducing a new person into your family life should be handled with care. As the parent, you set the guidelines for the role of the new adult—do you want them to provide financial support, discipline, teaching or fun? Once you marry, this marriage becomes the central relationship in the family, and everyone must adjust to that. Children at different ages will accept this differently, and older children can influence the younger children. Honest communication is vital for all concerned. Family meetings where everyone gets a say are helpful, and meeting rules (such as for every negative thing said, two positive things are said) provide focus and keep the conversation productive.

The bottom line? Take your time entering marriage, and be sure that this new person will enrich the life of your family emotionally, spiritually, and maybe even financially.

# HOBBIES

I believe the happiest people I know are people with hobbies. It doesn't seem to matter whether the hobby is woodworking or quilting, beading or building radios. When they are at their craft, their whole being is focused on the task at hand. Their creative juices are flowing. They are patient with their mistakes (well, maybe there's a little cussing from time to time), and persevere despite setbacks. They are pleased with their finished product, even though they are very aware of its flaws. They learn from the project and quickly move ahead with great new ideas. You can see these people at hardware stores and craft shops. You'll recognize them by the look of anticipation on their faces. **They'll probably be happy to chat with you about their next project. Feel free to ask.**

For us, as widow/ers, hobbies are a logical solution to those quiet hours that are so challenging. What if you've never had a hobby? Maybe you've been so busy taking care of everyone else and the budget has been so tight, that a hobby seemed like a pure luxury of both time and money. That was certainly the case for me. I thought the arts were for the rich, and that my time was best spent on making a living. My ideas about that evolved with a few experiences I've had. My late husband and I went to Johns Island in South Carolina on a mission trip to help the residents there with home repairs. The people who lived on this island, which was just about one foot above sea level, descended from slaves who were brought there from western Africa to work the rice plantations. While there, they entertained us after dinner one night by singing some old spirituals. It was like going back in time, to hear the same hymns in such authentic voice. Those people were financially poor, but the music created a spiritual wealth that no money could buy. The sharing of that music with us was an incredibly generous gift that I hold dear in my memory. Then, my Soup and Soul group from church watched a video that discussed Maya Angelou's *I Know Why the Caged Bird Sings*. That too brought home the concept that art is not just for those who can afford it, but for those who have nothing else. It is a path of self-exploration and self-expression that is not possible by any other means.

Another misconception I had about hobbies was that genetic talent was required. While that's partly true, I learned something from Heather Sepielli, an art student who lived with us for her first semester of college. At the time, she was studying perspective. She stayed up late into the night, drawing and re-drawing, with such persistence. She practiced using her eye as well as her hand. Though she had innate talent and desire, it still took a lot of hard work to satisfy her. I still get beautifully drawn Christmas cards from Heather, and I appreciate all the hard work behind each detail in each picture.

What's really important is to enjoy the activity. The finished project is secondary. Don't be critical of your effort. If you try and "fail," it's called learning. The next effort will be better. It will never be perfect. When I was making my first quilt, I took great pains to measure each cut, and to make each seam exactly the same size. But when I put the squares together, I still had to make adjustments. I called my friend Joyce Daubar, an experienced quilter, and asked, "Is it ever perfect?" She laughed, and said, "Never!" Someone else said that, "Perfect is the enemy of done."

So how do we choose a hobby? I'd like to concentrate on hobbies that you can do in your home during the quiet hours. Your quest for a hobby might start with a practical need. Maybe there are some household repairs that need to be done. Maybe there's furniture that needs to be refinished. Maybe there's a wall that needs a picture. Or it can be something less tangible. Is there a piano waiting to be used again? Is there a poem in your head waiting to be written? Are you interested in family history? Making a family tree is interesting. How about learning to edit photos and video on your computer?

**There are lots of classes available through craft stores and hardware stores. Definitely look into those**. Most of those classes are free, and offer great and practical information. Your town's adult education might offer classes that are affordable. Your newspaper might list a calendar that describes meetings of clubs on certain topics. You'll find quilting clubs and book clubs listed there. Then, there are all sorts of private lessons and academies for deeper exploration. I enjoyed tremendously a week-long class in mixed media at the John C. Campbell Folk Art School in North Carolina. This was my very first art class. I was honest about my inexperience, and humbly approached the learning process. The more experienced students and the teacher were most welcoming. They were actually joyful, knowing full well they were guiding me toward a great adventure. The young people tell me you can learn anything on YouTube. After taking a few classes, you might have some insight into what you enjoy. At worst, you'll have learned something that might be helpful someday.

Once you decide on a hobby, set up a dedicated place for it at home. You're more likely to engage in the activity if everything is set up and ready to go. In order to find this space, you may have to clear out some stuff you don't use anymore. Develop a list of supplies you'll need and get the things you absolutely need to get started. Then make a wish list for some nice extras. The list will make it easier for those who buy you gifts to select something you can use. Or, you can watch for those items to go on sale and get a good deal.

Your new hobby is a true adventure, and I'm excited for you as you begin!

# IS THERE A PET IN YOUR FUTURE?

By Lisa Saunders

(Note: Pets are very helpful for many people at every stage of life. I have never had a pet, so I asked my friend, Lisa, to share how having a pet helped her family through grieving the loss of her daughter. I hope you enjoy her insights.)

For those who live alone, a pet from a shelter may just be the perfect companion. "Dogs, cats, rabbits, horses, gerbils, birds, fish, and even reptiles can provide remarkable physical and psychological health benefits to humans," states Jack Hanna, director emeritus of the Columbus Zoo in Ohio and author of "Jack Hanna's Ultimate Guide to Pets."

"All pets reduce isolation and provide an object to receive love and care. As pets depend on their owner for basic survival needs, they provide the owner with an increased sense of purpose," says Julie Russell, MSW, LCSW-C, a psychological health professional in Washington, D.C.

I know from personal experience that a pet can even help in the grieving process after a major loss. When our daughter, Elizabeth, died at the age of 16, not only were my husband and I grieving, but Elizabeth's dog, Riley, grieved as well. He had spent the last five years of Elizabeth's life keeping her company on the couch. Elizabeth was quadriplegic and often ill, and since Riley didn't enjoy playing, they were very content resting companions. He was very gentle with Elizabeth and kept her cold feet warm by lying on them.

When Elizabeth died, it seemed as if Riley felt his purpose was gone. He no longer greeted us at the door nor would he lie on the couch to keep us company. He kept to himself in a corner of the house. Even so, having

Riley around felt like we still had a part of our daughter with us.

When he became terminally ill with cancer a year after Elizabeth died, Jim and I sat with him at the vet's office while Riley was put to sleep. We were inconsolable—it was as if Elizabeth died all over again. Our daily connection to her was gone. Jim stayed home from work that day and we went to bed in the early afternoon, too grief stricken to face the rest of the day.

Within a few hours of putting Riley down, our daughter, Jackie, who was away at college, found us a new pet. "Mom, it's not that I don't miss Riley, but I just found a dog who needs a home." He was a beagle/basset hound mix and had to live in a crate in his owner's kitchen because he wouldn't stop chasing her four cats.

Neither one of us wanted another dog. But did we really want Jackie to visit our home with both her sister and dog gone? We did not want our house to be viewed as a sad place. So, two days after Riley died, Jim and I drove to upstate New York to meet this hound. His owner said, "I feel so bad trying to find another home for him, but I just can't control him around my cats." I whispered to Jim, "He does make me laugh—we could use some of that." I was captured by his face. His eyes were somewhat saggy and sad, making me feel he understood my inner grief. We took him home that day.

To be honest, however, I didn't love Bailey at first—I kept comparing him to Riley who had been quiet, intelligent and obedient. Unlike Riley, Bailey was no couch potato. He was like having a noisy toddler underfoot. He pestered us to play in the evening when we just wanted to relax with the television. He barked and barked until we got off the couch and chased him around the house, pretending we were monsters after his squeaky toy. Other times, Bailey wanted us to kick a ball back and forth with him.

Our floors were strewn with toys we tripped over, and when we weren't home, he had accidents. He never listened when I asked him to sit or stay. When I asked the vet in a whisper at his first appointment if she thought he was kind of dumb, she replied, "No, he's just part basset hound and they do what they want, assuming you'll forgive them later."

A turning point in my feelings toward Bailey came one evening after asking Jim to take me home early from a party that reminded me too much of Elizabeth's passing—it was filled with people who had been very kind to our severely disabled little girl. Upon returning to our house, I wanted to crawl into bed and pull the covers over my head. But Bailey would have none of that—he barked at us until we gave in and clicked on his leash for a walk. As Jim and I discussed what a pain in the neck Bailey was, I thought of how he did at least distract us somewhat from our sorrow. Yes, Bailey was good for us. **Bailey demanded our attention and didn't care if we were too depressed to talk to him. He didn't want talking anyway, he**

**just wanted to be chased or walked. No matter what mood we were in, we were capable of doing that.**

Bailey was stylish, sporting cheerful bandanas. Bailey's woebegone expression and confusing breed mix caused the tourists in our town of Mystic, CT, to stop and ask what kind of dog he was. They asked if their children could pet Bailey and have their picture taken with him. It gave us great joy to watch little ones delight in Bailey's sloppy kisses and enthusiastic tail wagging. We had children back in our lives again—even if only for a moment.

On pets and grieving, Russell says, "The relationship with a pet is unique. While a pet will not replace the loss of a loved one, it provides a reason for continuing to get out of bed and move forward in life. A pet is dependent on its owner and in turn generally thankful and not judgmental. This makes a pet a good individual to talk to."

Hanna suggests in his book that learning the pros and cons of the kind of animal you wish to consider will help you determine "how much pleasure/comfort/company a pet will give you versus how much work/space/time it will take for you to enjoy it." You can learn about the realities of pet care through books, animal shelters, vets, pet store owners, and the **American Society for the Prevention of Cruelty to Animals** (ASPCA). For those not ready to take on a pet, Russell suggests volunteering in animal shelters.

I wish I had consulted my local animal shelter first before inviting a long list of unsuitable pets into our home. We tried a hamster, but it bored Jackie and my fear of rodents made cleaning the cage challenging. A kitten scratched Elizabeth's face. A rabbit did nothing but stink up its cage.

I found Hanna's book on pets very enlightening as it outlined the personality traits and requirements of standard pets such as cats, dogs and birds, along with the not-so-standard pets like rats, pot-bellied pigs and even cockroaches. For example, I was surprised by Hanna's statement, "A bird can be as much of a buddy as a dog, as playful and cuddly as a kitten— and as obnoxious as a toddler with a tantrum."

I know a lot of people who love the ease of caring for a cat, and they take pleasure in watching their goofy antics. My friend Cindy Modzelewski of Virginia faced loneliness when she moved away from her home in Connecticut. It was her kitty who gave her a reason to smile: "Misty has the softest, fluffiest fur and is a good company keeper—she even likes to sit in the bathroom sink when I'm brushing my teeth! She loves to rub noses, especially when I'm trying to put in my contact lenses."

Regarding reptiles, however, I found it hard to believe anyone could have feelings toward them until I asked a teenager who owned both a snake and a lizard. He replied, "Yes, I love them. They are very cute and you become very attached to them." Snakes and lizards cute? Maybe there really is a pet for everyone!

To decide if pet adoption is right for you, start with the ASPCA's webpage on the questions you should ask yourself. Click on: http://www.aspca.org/adopt/adoption-tips/questions-ask-yourself-adopting.

# FAITH

The Jesuits say, "Give me a child until he is seven, and I'll give you the man." The faith of our childhood is woven into our tapestry whether we like it or not. Some of us accept and embrace the teachings, questioning little because it works for us. The community and rituals are comforting and meaningful. Others reject the faith traditions of their families outright. But even the rejection has an energy that influences us. And then there are many who are not raised within any faith tradition. So we come to this time in our lives, when we can decide for ourselves how to practice our spirituality. I recommend that you take some time to examine your faith practices. Continue to take joy in those aspects that are meaningful to you, and try some new approaches.

I love the term "faith journey." Journey isn't used to describe a quick trip or even a vacation. It implies a long path with unexpected encounters. Our faith is like that. Sometimes everything is clear and we move forward confidently; other times, there's a fog and we can't make any sense of anything. There are times when the going is easy, and at other times the road is straight uphill. There are times when we travel alone, and times when we are surrounded in good company. When we look back, we'll see that every aspect of the journey had a lesson for us. If we pay attention, we'll find a very interesting story.

The most common complaint about this stage of life is the quiet in the house. However, that quiet is the perfect environment for pursuing spiritual growth. Is it coincidence that when we need our faith the most, the perfect environment presents itself?

## Meditation

Meditation is a practice common to all faith traditions. It's also recommended by most physicians as a healthy way to reduce the negative effects of stress. It is a discipline that takes practice, though there are many "right" ways to do it. The tradition is to sit cross legged on the carpeted floor, with hands resting palm up on the knees. But if that is not comfortable for you, you can sit any way you choose. The room should be free of distractions, though meditative music may be on. Some people use an icon to focus on. Others chant a mantra or a word that centers them. Breathe deeply and slowly. Focus on your breathing. If stray thoughts come into your head, observe that the thought is there and then let it go. Go back to focusing on your breathing. Continue for five, 10 or 20 minutes, and repeat daily.

Be patient with yourself. Most of us experience "monkey brain" when we first begin. You'll find after some experience that the time passes more quickly, and that you feel refreshed afterwards. In time, this meditation can be prayerful and you may feel a connection to God. Our days are typically so noisy that it's hard for God to get a word to us. Meditation is our time to rest and to listen.

## Labyrinth

If you find sitting still is difficult, try walking a labyrinth. You can find one near you by consulting labyrinthlocator.com. Labyrinths are found all over the world, some dating back 3000 years. They predate today's religions, but are located on sites that seem to have spiritual significance. They were adopted by the Roman Catholic Church during the 1200s, and you'll find them built into the floors of Europe's cathedrals. At that time, walking a labyrinth was a metaphor for a pilgrimage to the Holy Land. The most famous is an 11-circuit labyrinth in the Cathedral of Chartres, just outside Paris. There is its replica outdoors at Grace Cathedral in San Francisco. At first glance, it may look like a maze, but you'll soon see that there are no barriers. Your only decision is to enter. But before you do, stop and think for a minute. Is there something you'd like to get rid of, like guilt or anger? Or is there something you'd like to seek clarity on? Or is there a creative block you'd like to move past? If so, use that issue as an intention for your walk. Then clear your mind, take a deep breath and start your walk.

You'll take lots of twists and turns. You'll think you're almost to the center, and then the path brings you back out. You'll see lots of metaphors for your issue along the way. It will take about 10 minutes to get to the center, depending on your pace and the size of the labyrinth. Once in the center, you may stand, sit, or kneel. But wait for a few minutes until you feel at peace or inspired, or forgiven, or whatever it is that you're seeking. Then walk back out, the same way as you came in. The idea is re-enter the same world but as a new person.

**Classical Seven Circuit Labyrinth**

## Learning about Faith

Sometimes, faith in action is a good way to re-enter the world of faith. Habitat for Humanity builds homes with the future residents of the house. In their offices and on their worksites, you'll find people of all denominations of faith. You'll find other faithful people working in homeless shelters and soup kitchens, and delivering meals to the homebound. They may not preach, but they are living the Word as they understand it. Being in the company of people of faith allows you to explore some ideas without being confronted with evangelism. Once you get to know someone whom you admire, you can ask questions about their faith. Don't be surprised if they invite you to their house of worship. You may decline if you wish; just say you're not ready yet.

You might consider taking a course online or at a local college about world religions. The library will also have a section on this topic. If you don't have a faith tradition, it would be a good way to get an overview. You will find many commonalities among the world religions. What may differ is the culture that surrounds them, or on the difference in emphasis on different aspects of the faith.

## Joining a Faith Community

Why might you decide to join a faith community? Well, if you've ever watched a campfire, you know that the sticks that are piled properly burn well. A stick that falls away, even if it's burning well at first, will quickly extinguish itself. A faith community provides an environment that stokes our fire. It provides opportunities for learning theology and the history of the practice and traditions of the faith.[9]

Look for a community that welcomes newcomers. Look for opportunities for small group study. Look for opportunities for service together. Many churches also offer social opportunities like dinners. The theology should be a tool to build your understanding of God and to help you to develop your personal relationship with God. The theology should also support our relationships with one another so that we live in harmony and justice. There is no faith community that will be 100% perfect, because communities are made of people. But a good faith community should allow for human frailty without too much angst. Be prepared to be forgiving and to be forgiven.

If you're perfectly happy with your childhood faith traditions, certainly consider going back. It may take a while to feel at home there again, but make the effort.

If you don't have a church home, perhaps you weren't raised in a church, or your spouse wasn't comfortable in your faith tradition or maybe something in your experience turned you off. Widower-hood is a stage of life when we certainly seek meaning and a connection to our spirituality. For many of us, exploring options for faith development helps with every aspect of our lives.

Trying out new houses of worship can be fun. Try several different churches/temples. Keep a journal so you can remember your impressions. If there's one you like, attend each week for a month or so. Then watch for opportunities to become involved in the activities that occur during the week. Watch for places where your talents meet the congregation's needs. A congregation needs a great variety of talents to function. They need people in building maintenance, communication, finance, social leadership, teaching, hospitality, music, and so many other areas. You will definitely find a niche that suits you. Someone who is willing to pitch in is always welcome. You'll find you get a lot out of the Sunday worship service, and you'll double the effect when you live in community with your fellow congregants. Most people stay with a congregation because of relationships

---

[9] Idea from sermon by Rev. Robert Moore. Niantic Community Church. Niantic, CT

with others.

The house of worship that you choose to join should foster your faith development, should help you live in harmony with those you love and with new friends, and should offer opportunities for socializing and providing service in community.

Etiquette varies in different congregations, and knowing these traditions might ease your entry. In all, dress conservatively and respectfully. Turn off your cell phone. Refrain from eating, drinking and talking during the service.

When visiting a Jewish temple or shul, Robert Levin, MD, advises women to wear a simple head covering. Only Jewish men wear a fringed prayer shawl called a tallit, but Yarmulkes will be available for visiting men. The worship leader is a rabbi (teacher). No collection plate is passed on the Sabbath. The Torah is a book stored in an Ark (the Aron Kodesh). Do not leave the sanctuary while the ark is open. See *Jewish Literacy*[10] for more information.

Govind Menon, PhD, advises that when visiting a Hindu temple, the traditional greeting is *Namaste,* which translates: "I honor the spirit in you which is also in me," said with palms together at chest height, with a slight bow to the shrine. Remove shoes before entering the sanctuary. While seated, either sit with your legs folded beneath you or pointed away from the shrine. It is customary to leave a gift of $1 to $5 toward the upkeep of the temple in a specially marked box. The worship leader, called a Priest, Pandit or Pujari, is addressed as "Swamiji". At the end of a prayer service, the pujari may offer some of the items (flowers, fruit or nuts) used in the service to visitors. Always accept these and any other items offered only with your right hand.

When visiting a Muslim temple, remove shoes before entering. Women wear head coverings. Men and women may use different entrances. It is traditional for a woman to wait until a man extends his hand in greeting. Do not walk in front of someone who is praying. The traditional greeting is "Salaam alaykum" (Peace be upon you) and the response is "Wa alykum salaam" (And upon you peace).

A Roman Catholic mass lasts about 45 minutes and consists of hymns, opening prayers, prayers of contrition and for the needs of the people, readings from the Bible, a sermon, collection basket for voluntary donations and Holy Communion. Communion is offered to practicing Catholics, but visitors are often invited forward for a blessing. There are times to sit, stand, and kneel. Don't sit in the front pew, so that you can follow those seated in front of you. There will be a printed program with

---

[10] Telushkin Rabbi Joseph. Jewish Literacy. Morow & Co. 1991.

prayers and responses, usually in the pew. There will be a time to offer peace to those seated nearby. You may shake hands or bow slightly, saying, "Peace of Christ be with you;" the response is, "And also with you". The worship leader is often a priest, called, "Father".

A Protestant service, also Christian, will often follow a format similar to the Roman Catholic mass. All are welcome to receive communion. The worship leader is titled, Reverend and called "Pastor".

I practice my faith now in a Protestant church, but I was raised in the Roman Catholic tradition. When I was small, I learned the Roman Catholic Baltimore Catechism. **Question number 6** was: Why did God make you? **Answer:** God made me to know Him, to love Him, and to serve Him in this world, and to be happy with Him forever in the next.

Even at the age of six, I was given the understanding that this life was intended to be finite. And, there would continue to be joy in the next life. That perspective has made the acceptance of death a little easier for me. (I can still get angry about it; don't get me wrong–but I understand that it was the deal from the start.)

A word of caution: A cult is a group that focuses on controlling people though reverence for the worship leader. True religions emphasize our relationship with God, and respect the concept of free will.

I hope you find a faith community that will provide a sense of peace with God, and the support and companionship of open hearted people.

*I have not lost faith in God. I have moments of anger and protest. Sometimes I've been closer to him for that reason.*

Elie Wiesel

# HEALTH

Good health has the reward of a sense of well-being. It is waking up feeling well-rested, with anticipation and readiness for all the great stuff that will happen that day. It's the capacity to tolerate disappointments, to perform work and hobbies, and to problem solve. Our body just knows how to do so many things automatically. We breathe, swallow, eat, and chemically regulate all of our systems without much conscious effort. Many of us can get by for a long time without contributing to the automatic control. Still, it's critical to know that stress, grief and other challenges can hamper our body's natural defenses. That's why this is a good time to take inventory of our health so we can intervene if there's something we can do to make life easier for our bodies.

First of all, how did you sleep last night? Sleep is of paramount importance for all of our systems: physical, emotional and spiritual. Sleep is when we process memory. If you find yourself being forgetful, it may be a symptom of insomnia.

There are physical causes of insomnia. Hormones can cause insomnia, especially among women during menopause. Sometimes, insomnia is a symptom of sleep apnea; this is interrupted breathing, followed by a snorting snore when breathing resumes. Sleep apnea needs to be treated by a physician

More often, insomnia is caused by worry, and low level, chronic anxiety keeps us from getting into REM sleep. REM sleep is when our muscles completely relax and heal from the day's work. People who don't get into REM sleep often suffer chronic muscular pain like fibromyalgia. We can also just feel drowsy during the day when we haven't slept well. It's difficult to pay attention and we may fall asleep while driving. My social worker says that if I have a recurring thought that keeps me awake, it's my brain's way of trying to remember it. It helped a lot when I followed her advice to write down what was on my mind. Once it was written, I no longer had to remember it. Some people self-treat insomnia with alcohol. That bottle of sherry on the bedside table may help them fall asleep, but oftentimes, several hours later, they wake fully, and have trouble getting back to sleep. Some people turn to sleep medications, which can be appropriate, but you don't want to become dependent on them, so keep in touch with your doctor if you're using medications to sleep.

If insomnia is a problem for you, I encourage you to make sleep a priority. You really can't progress in other aspects of your life if you're not sleeping well. When I was in college, a professor looked into our bleary eyes during an 8:00 class on a Friday morning, and said, "You can't soar with the eagles when you've been hooting with the owls." So true! There are physicians who specialize in sleep disorders. Find one at your local hospital. Don't delay.

It's well established that people who are married live longer than those who live single. The reasons why this is true are less well defined. If we were a primary caregiver for our spouse for years, we may not have gone for our own annual check-ups, and missed finding a problem early. Perhaps single people have less income, and so don't have access to the same quality of health care as married people do. Or, maybe it's because there's no one to give us the nudge to exercise, or to get some little symptom checked out. Perhaps it's because we eat differently.

The stress of being widowed also takes a toll on our emotional health. We might experience loneliness, the blues, or depression. We may worry about things over which we have no control. We may stay in a state of heightened alert if we don't always feel safe. We may harbor anger about our spouse' death, especially if there was violence or malpractice involved. We may hold grudges about things that happened. We may feel guilty over not being perfect spouses. Sometimes it just feels as though we can't control so much of what is so important.

What is it that you're holding in that impacts your emotional health?

It's important to define it so that you can deal with it. Many issues can be dealt with by talking with a friend or another widow/er. I have gotten great consolation by talking with my in-laws. My late husband's brother was able to proxy for his brother in forgiving some things I felt guilty about. His reassurance was incredibly helpful. You know that there are groups for grieving as well. But if a problem impairs your ability to sleep or function, talk with a professional psychologist or social worker. You can ask for references at the local Hospice or from your family practice doctor. Resolving the issue at hand will free up your brain to work on more interesting ideas. A brain under stress does not think clearly and is not a good problem solver.

And while we're on mental health, I want to assure you that it's okay to be happy. In fact, it's not a sign of respect for our loved one to be miserable.

Longevity is not the only factor in assessing the quality of one's health. I think the impact of health on our quality of life is more important. We want to be healthy enough to live independently and to enjoy new opportunities that present themselves. We want to spend our disposable income on fun, not on medicine.

Our health also impacts our families. We don't want to be a burden to our children.

So what must we do to stay healthy? It starts with caring about your health. It's so easy to be sloppy. There has to be a real reason to want to be healthy. For me, it started when my first grandchild was expected. I wanted to be able to play on the floor, and to run and swim together. I didn't want to be the family member everyone had to wait for because I couldn't keep up. So about five years ago, 6 months before my first grandchild was born, I joined Anytime Fitness. This is a national franchise gym that is open 24/7. So there was no excuse for not finding time. After meeting with Axel Mahlke, personal trainer, I started just with exercise for 3 months. When the work-out started to become easy, I met with Rosemary Collins, the registered dietician on staff at Anytime Fitness. She asked me to keep a food journal for 2 weeks. When we met to review the journal, she helped me set goals (one pound a week for 10 weeks). I was heavy, but I didn't really think that I could ever be thin. Even to lose a little would be helpful. To meet that goal, at my age and height, I cut down to 1200 calories per day. I used the computer program to document my food intake and my activity level. Sure enough, I lost one pound a week for 10 weeks. Then I wondered if maybe I could continue. It wasn't too hard. I had the routine down now. So I continued on until I lost 50 pounds, and I've kept it off for 5 years. I went from a size 16 to a size 6. But more importantly, I met my goal of being able to play with my grandchild. I was thrilled beyond all expectations when we skied together! (Yes, a very slight incline at the "magic sidewalk," but still skiing!) So I had motivation from becoming a grandmother and my reward is being able to play. You'll find your motivating factor.

When you're ready, and I hope it's very soon, start by choosing a primary care physician. Asking people who work in the medical field for recommendations is a good way to find a physician who will take time to be thorough and to answer your questions. Schedule an appointment for a complete physical. Be very honest about your lifestyle, your emotional health, and your symptoms. Ask which tests are appropriate for someone your age. Get the tests that are ordered. Then go back for a follow-up visit to review the results of the tests. Ask for referrals to specialists as needed. For example, if your cholesterol is high, ask for a consult with a registered dietician. If you have insomnia, ask to see a sleep specialist. If you have arthritis, ask to see a physical therapist. Ask if you have any restrictions on exercise. Ask about vaccinations that are recommended. Bring a notebook with you to all your appointments. Prior to your appointments, write down your questions, then jot down the advice you're given and follow through. Write your plan. Keep your motivation in mind.

Here's a chart to help you stay focused at your appointments:

### Path to Good Health

| Consultant | Advice | Strategy | Date | Accountability |
|------------|--------|----------|------|----------------|
|            |        |          |      |                |
|            |        |          |      |                |
|            |        |          |      |                |
|            |        |          |      |                |

Even though we may live alone, it's easy to find groups to support our healthy lifestyle. There are certainly gyms available. Some, like Anytime Fitness are open 24/7, allowing great flexibility of work-out times. Towns offer classes though Parks and Rec, and there is often great variety offered, from yoga to Zumba. Community pools offer lap swims and aerobic exercise classes. Military bases have great work-out facilities. There are outside options as well. The Appalachian Mountain Club offers hikes in addition to kayaking and travel. Use MeetUp.com to find locals who share your interests. But you know all this already, don't you? Don't be shy. At each of these places, there are people ready to welcome you, to orient you to the activity, and to encourage you. If you try one place and don't like it, try someplace else. Many offer a free trial period. It won't be long before you find your exercise home.

Dental care is more important than you'd think. Research shows that much of the body's inflammation develops in the mouth. Most dental insurances cover preventive care, so there is no good reason for not seeing your dentist regularly. Following through with instructions regarding flossing and ultrasonic brushing will help prevent the more expensive procedures that are not covered by insurance. Think of it this way: If it takes 5 minutes a day to floss and brush properly, that's 30 hours per year. With a crown costing $3000, that payoff is $100 per hour for your time! That's value. A dentist can also help with emotional health. Who wants to smile with chipped or yellowing front teeth? And it's hard to make friends when you don't smile.

Vision is the last item on your health check list. Good vision is important for driving safely and for preventing falls; yet, it can change so gradually, you might not notice it. And there are many eye conditions that can be treated if recognized early. Eye exams are typically covered by insurance. So be sure to see a qualified optometrist or ophthalmologist regularly.

Though it may seem time consuming, the rewards of good health are worth the effort. You'll waken feeling rested, with energy and comfort. Your posture will reflect your positive outlook on life. You'll increase your quality of life as you are able to be more active.

# EMOTIONAL HEALTH

Eric Lindermann was the first psychiatrist and psychologist who analyzed what a surviving spouse must do in order to adjust after their loss. In addition to the traditional forms of grieving, he added the task of reconstruction of the self-concept and the widow's various identities in relationships with others. He noted that while there was community support for the early stages of grief, the widow/er was left alone to try to re-establish his or her identity. [11] It takes an intentional analysis of who we are in our work, our families, and in our communities to understand ourselves at this stage of life. This is a time to decide how we feel about the identities we have established, and what we might want to change.

**We're most prone to mistakes when we are not in good emotional health.** It's so easy to get stuck in anger, sadness, guilt, or anxiety, that we can't think straight. Anger can be directed at our spouse, who smoked or was careless with his or her diet. If there was violence involved in the death, there may certainly be anger at the perpetrator. And it if was suicide, there may be a mix of anger and guilt. If it's a military death, we may just be mad at the whole country. When we're angry, we might speak without care for others. We end up alienating the people we need the most.

**We may also feel guilty for all sorts of things.** How about the times we were less than perfect spouses? (Come on, now, who was a perfect spouse?!) Or if we caused the death through an accident, the guilt could be overwhelming. Although I left the Roman Catholic Church years ago, their

---

[11] Linderman, Eric. Symptomology and Management of Acute grief. American Journal of Psychiatry 101 (1944):141-148.

concept of the sacrament of confession has benefit in this situation. There is something to be said for saying out loud that you're sorry and for being granted forgiveness. If you are suffering from guilt, I urge you to seek some sort of peace with it. You can't undo what is done. But maybe you can channel that energy to prevent the same thing happening to someone else. Also, seek groups of people who are in the same situation. There are groups for survivor families of suicide deaths and for those killed by drunk drivers. Another form of guilt is survivor guilt. Why my spouse and not me? There is no good answer to this. It doesn't help to dwell on it. But sometimes, just the underlying feeling places some pressure on us to perform. I try to use it as an energy source to live fully.

**Feeling helpless or overwhelmed is a common response (especially among men) to grief.** Unfortunately, these emotions can make us vulnerable to predators, from high-pressure sales people to fraudulent requests for your credit card information. So it's a good idea at such times to stop and think. Most decisions can be deferred to a later time. Try to be very specific about the issue at hand. Defining the problem helps us start developing a solution. Consider the pros and cons of all your options. Be careful when you feel incompetent—reach out and ask somebody you know and trust to review the situation with you. Never yield to pressure to follow someone's advice. Be sure to understand the rationale for making decisions, and maintain control of the things that you care about.

**Sadness can become a habit.** We've experienced a huge disappointment. Many of our hopes and dreams, and our sense of security have been stripped. It's perfectly understandable to be sad. Men tend to suffer more depression than women. For many men, their wife was their only confidant, and she buffered him from many of the stresses in his life. (I didn't realize that I was holding onto sadness like this until I started going to the gym. After working out for 6 months, I started to notice a spring in my step. I said to the trainer, "Wow–it feels good to have a spring in my step again!") There's a whole body language to sadness. The head is down, the spine and shoulders are rounded. Walking pace is slow, with minimal trunk rotation. No one is going to approach someone who looks like that with a broad smile and a friendly hello. If you can, try to control at least your physical posture. Dr. Phil says that we teach people how to treat us. If we have a sad demeanor, people will either ignore us, or will match our mood. Neither does us any good. Presenting a positive image will attract more positive social interaction, which in turn, will cheer us up. I give you permission to be cheerful—so you should too! As soon as you are able, find friends who make you laugh. Watch fun movies. Get out in the fresh air. Be happy.

**Anxiety can be paralyzing.** When we lose our spouse, the rug has been pulled out from under us, and there's a big hole in the floor. We are off balance, we don't know where it's safe to step. The easiest thing to do is to wrap up in a blanket on the couch and stay there for long periods of time. And the longer we're there, the scarier the world gets. When we keep ourselves isolated like that, we lose touch with our social circle. Loneliness increases. It's a downward spiral that is very hard to reverse. The fears are both real and exaggerated; either way, the exaggerated fears feel as if they were real. Solving this dilemma takes some self-talk. I bought a sign that I display in my hallway. It's a quote from Christopher Robbin to Winnie the Pooh, and it says, "Promise me you'll always remember that you're braver than you believe, and stronger than you seem, and smarter than you think."

The late wife of Joe's cousin is a competent woman whom I admire greatly. I called her one day, and said, "Annie Lee, do you ever get tired of being brave?" She laughed and said, "Oh, yes!" Being brave takes a lot of energy. But don't feel that you have to do it alone. People really do want to help you; they just don't know how. Try to be specific with people. If someone invites you to a movie, don't say no because you're afraid to drive at night. Say, I'd love to, but would you mind picking me up? And at the end of the evening, if you don't like entering a dark house alone, leave the lights and radio on. Start with the little things and your confidence will build with successes.

**An emotion that's not mentioned too often is jealousy.** As we sit around a table of women and they talk about how their husbands fix things, manage the finances, and get the show tickets, we are reminded that it's all on us. If we don't change the light bulb, pay the bills, and arrange the entertainment, it doesn't get done. And should a husband happen to drop in, and kiss his wife…well, sometimes, that can be tough. Or how about when a co-worker gets flowers on Valentine's Day? Or when another couple takes that special vacation that you had hoped to take someday? Those moments are real and can set us back a bit. I try to counter jealousy by counting the blessings I do have—a table full of friends to start with, and the ability to do some minor repairs myself and buy my own movie ticket.

If you've made a mistake, take some time for self-reflection or enlist the help of a trusted friend. Be careful not to jump from a particular issue, like spending too much on a birthday gift, to a generalization like, "I can't manage money." The more concretely you can pinpoint the issue and understand what you've done wrong, the more you can make appropriate adjustments toward a more positive path. What makes this possible is for us to have compassion for ourselves. The best advice is, "Don't be too hard on yourself." Look at the situation as objectively as you can. Imagine that it wasn't you who made the mistake, but a friend. Treat yourself as you would treat a friend who had made that mistake. Use humor. Be kind. Remember that failure is just a step toward learning.

# REGAIN YOUR EMOTIONAL HEALTH

All of the emotions described above are perfectly normal immediately after the death of your spouse and some may continue to surface from time to time. But it's wise to learn strategies to quickly recognize when they start to emerge, and control their influence over your current life. Otherwise, it's easy to get stuck in these emotional states. Getting stuck is a problem because it leaves you vulnerable to making errors in judgment. Seek whatever help you need to work through the feelings that are holding you back.

### Behavioral Health

When we are in good emotional health, we spend our time in activities that are interesting to us and bring us a sense of joy and satisfaction. We choose to be with people who encourage us to be our best selves, who support us in our efforts, and who want us to be happy. Sometimes, such as after the loss of a spouse, we go through stages of poor emotional health. During those times, we are vulnerable to spending our time in ways that do not move us forward very well. Sometimes, we spend time with other people who are not productive in any sense, but we can get pulled into their lifestyle behaviors such as gambling, alcohol or drug use. Those behaviors might feel good initially, providing an escape from our blues—that initial good feeling is what keeps us coming back. But most of us recognize that these behaviors won't give us long term happiness. The best strategy, of course, is to not get started on them in the first place. But once in, there are strategies for coming back to health. I've asked some experts to help me discuss these topics.

# Gambling

*By gambling we lose both our time and treasure: two things most precious to the life of man.*

Owen Feltham(1602-1668; English essay writer)

When that life insurance check comes in, it sure looks like a lot of money! It makes us feel confident about our financial situation. So if we're looking to get out of our quiet house and to be around people, a trip to the casino might seem the perfect pastime. However, casinos are masters at making lonely people feel comfortable. There are active games like poker and roulette, and games that require more skill than luck, like slot machines or bingo. There is also easy access to alcohol. This leads about 3% of American adults to develop a moderate to severe gambling problem. Numbers are rising more quickly among women than among men. Women tend to prefer slot machines, which have a fast speed of play. The faster the wager to response time, the more likely it is to develop a problem.[12] Moreover, according to the New York Times, of all addictive behaviors, gambling has the highest rate of suicide. [13]

Maureen O'Connor was a Catholic school teacher and mayor of San Diego. She lost her husband in 1994. As he was the founder of the fast-food hamburger chain, Jack-in-the Box, she received an inheritance in excess of $40 million. I'm sure she felt that she would be comfortable for the rest of her life. In 2000, she began gambling at casinos throughout the country. Soon, she found herself unable to stop, citing the grief over losing her husband as one reason. She lost her entire inheritance, and then even more. Although she sold her jewelry, a home, an art collection, and a hotel, she was still unable to pay her debts. She finally hit bottom when she stole $2 million from a charitable foundation that her late husband had established. For that she was charged with a federal crime and was incarcerated.

Mary Sojourner describes a widow who committed suicide because she felt that she could not dig out from under her gambling debts. Her distraught daughter found her lying dead on the living room couch. There was an empty bottle of antidepressants next to her and a folder on the floor. The folder contained a list of 11 credit cards, each with a balance over $5,000. On the front of the folder she had written, "I'm so sorry." The

[12] Department of Mental Health and Addiction Services, Problem Gambling Services, State of Connecticut.

[13] http://nytimes.com/1997/12/16/us/suicide-rate-higher-in-3-gambling-cities-study-says.html

daughter further learned that her mother had gambled away all her savings, the investments that she had inherited from her husband, and the bank was about to foreclose on the house.[14]

Problem gambling can develop in anyone. It does not discriminate against gender, age, social or economic groups. These 10 questions have been developed to help individuals determine whether they have a gambling problem.

Please take a moment and answer these questions faithfully:

1. Have you been preoccupied with thoughts of gambling while doing other things?
2. Have you been restless or irritable when unable to gamble?
3. Have you hidden your gambling from family members?
4. Has gambling created conflict and unhappiness in your life?
5. Have you tried to stop gambling but have not been able to?
6. Have you gambled to obtain money to pay debts or solve other financial problems?
7. Have you needed someone else to bail you out of a gambling debt?
8. Have you ever borrowed money and not paid it back as a result of your gambling?
9. Have you been unable to pay bills due to a gambling loss?
10. Have you ever thought you might have a gambling problem?

If you answered yes to any of these questions, you may seek information and guidance at the Connecticut Council on Problem Gambling Helpline: 1-800-34NO BET. The Council's website, ccpg.org is another source of free, confidential information.

## Are You Drowning in Your Sorrow?[15]

By Jane Milardo, LFMT

Are you drowning in sorrow and loss? The death of a spouse, whether expected or not, changes everything from your future plans and financial stability to the way you sleep, eat, and get on with the everyday chores of life.

You wake up alone. You figure out how to do the things your spouse used to do. Your mail still arrives with your spouse's name attached. You explain to people who haven't seen you recently what has happened, sometimes over and over again. You face the next big holiday, and then the

---

[14] Sojourner Mary. She Bets her Life. Seals Press. 2010.

[15] Milardo Jane. Are You Drowing your Sorrow? Pathfinder: a Companion Guide for the Widow/er's Journey. Vol 1 No 5: 43-46.

next after that, without your spouse. So many adjustments, big and small, wash over you in waves, and if you haven't had time to plan or prepare for them—or sometimes even if you have—they can make you sink into a depression.

Grieving after a loss is normal, but if you find yourself unable to get out of bed in the morning or to function through the day, if you're experiencing changes in appetite or sleep habits, difficulty concentrating, low energy, an excessive amount of guilt, or inability to care about anything, you may be clinically depressed. If this sounds like you, seek the help of a licensed therapist who can help you recover from depression and process your emotional issues.

In a time of deep sorrow, it's not uncommon to have a drink to forget, to numb emotions, to cope, or to sleep. You may stop at the bar on the way home to be in the company of others or to avoid being home too long. You may begin to drink at home, in isolation. But if you find yourself drinking more often, or if you become aware that you are gradually drinking more, you may be trying to drown your sorrow in alcohol.

Having done substance abuse recovery work for years, I am amazed both by what most people don't know about alcohol and by what some people think they know about alcohol, but don't really. I have seen the same patterns over and over again. You don't see alcohol dependence coming. Alcohol is a sneaky substance in that, as you drink more for whatever reason, there comes a tipping point where you lose track of how much you have consumed and just continue drinking. Although you may not be aware of your pattern of drinking more, gradually it begins to impact your life in negative ways. That's why I feel it's imperative to share some facts about alcohol.

Who is an alcoholic? An alcoholic is someone who has become physically dependent on alcohol. Alcoholics crave alcohol, think about it often, and look forward to their next drink. Alcohol becomes their best friend, but then it begins to disrupt and dominate their life in a number of different ways, including developing family, legal, work, or health problems.

There are many myths about alcohol, so let's get the stories straight. Not all alcoholics are bums in the street. Most are average people who think they are normal drinkers. Not all alcoholics drink every day; some are binge drinkers. They may drink only on weekends, but they drink to oblivion. It's not true that you can't be an alcoholic if you "only" drink wine or beer. Wine and beer contain plenty of alcohol and are as addictive as any other form. Wine connoisseurs are just as vulnerable to addiction as anyone else. Just because it's rare or expensive doesn't mean it's any safer in large quantities.

Some of the early signs of an alcohol problem include blackouts (not remembering all or part of what happened while you were under the influence), family arguments about your drinking, nausea, vomiting, and an increased tolerance for large quantities of alcohol. If you can drink a lot of alcohol without feeling drunk, it means that you have developed more tolerance and are closer to becoming addicted. If other people express concern about your drinking, chances are that you are abusing alcohol.

Since alcohol addiction is a gradual process, you may not be aware of the problem, so you ought to trust that if your loved ones and others are all saying the same thing about your drinking, you need to address the problem. If you have had a DUI, domestic incident or other legal problem that involves alcohol, then it is surely a problem for you. If all your friends are heavy drinkers, you may want to reconsider the company you are keeping. If you are losing friends because of your drinking, it is a problem. If you fall and injure yourself while drinking, it is a problem.

Never drink to escape from an emotional problem. That is called self-medicating behavior. Those times when you are grieving, angry, overwhelmed, or under stress are the worst times to drink, because not only are you more likely to drink too much, but you are not doing any real problem-solving in regard to the issue. And guess what? When you sober up, the problem will still be there. The longer you self-medicate a problem, the fewer coping skills you develop toward solving it. Instead, you create a vicious cycle that, if allowed to continue, can result in addiction.

Make no mistake about it. Alcohol is a drug, and it is an addictive drug. Since it happens to be legal, people mistakenly see using it as harmless or "normal" adult behavior, a rite of passage, if you will. Since alcohol is addictive, you should always handle it with care. You wouldn't play with fire as if it is harmless. Why would you play with alcohol?

If you choose to drink, ALWAYS be aware of how many drinks you take. If they're mixed drinks, make sure you know how many shots they contain. Pay attention to how many drinks it takes to make you feel inebriated, and next time stop prior to that point. That is responsible drinking.

NEVER drink shots, a dangerous behavior that can lead to alcohol poisoning. Never allow others to continue to buy you or pour drinks you haven't asked for. You can refuse them and say, "Thanks anyway, but no." That is responsible drinking.

Remember also that you will be drunk long before you feel drunk. That's why some people insist on driving, even though those around them can see that they are inebriated. If your goal in drinking is to become as drunk as possible, you may have a problem.

Ask yourself these questions: "Why do I need to be in an altered state of mind?" "What do I need to escape from? "What feelings am I masking?" You have to face your problems before you can solve them.

It's okay to cry, to be angry (as long as you don't take it out on someone), scared, or insecure about living without your spouse. Find someone who will listen and talk with you about it. Sometimes friends or relatives want to help but they don't know how, so they can offer only sympathy. A widow/widowers' support group can do wonders because you are in contact with other people who share your feelings and the reasons for those feelings. Some of them can become lifelong friends. It's also comforting to know that you're not alone.

If you're uncomfortable in a support group, see a professional counselor who can help you through the process of change. If, in reading this chapter, you recognize yourself as a problem drinker, don't hesitate to go to Alcoholics Anonymous, where people understand, don't judge, and know how to help. There is definitely hope. People recover all the time.

Don't drown in your sorrows. Face your challenges, accept the help that's offered, and ask for help if you need it. Do not fear. Change is part of life, and it can be good. Be open to changes and see what they have to offer you.

*Calm mind brings inner strength and self-confidence, so that's very important for good health.*

Dalai Lama

# FRIENDSHIP

*A friend is someone who bails you out of jail at midnight. A best friend is the one sitting beside you in the cell, saying, "Wow, that was so much fun!"*

There are times when the need for friends is so obvious. Hopefully, we won't need to be bailed out of jail, but that would certainly be near the top of the list. On a more typical day, we need friends for companionship, for feedback on ideas, for laughter, and for validation. It takes time to develop a true friendship. The shared experiences help build trust. There are all sorts of ways to look at friendship, but I learned the most about it from the most unlikely sources.

At work one day as a physical therapist, I was stretching the hamstrings of a 10 year old girl. She was a very cute child with a big, winning smile; she was also mentally disabled, unable to speak, and used a wheelchair to get around. Lying next her on the exercise mat was another 10 year old girl, whom I'll call Sally. Sally was born with a cleft palate and without legs, and was also non-verbal. As I stretched my little patient's leg, she winced a bit. Sally reached out and took my patient's hand. They made eye contact and smiled. I was flabbergasted, because I thought that both girls lacked the mental capacity to experience empathy. I learned a lesson that day I'll never forget—the key to friendship is to simply be present with empathy.

With loneliness being the biggest problem we face, friends become more important than ever. In times of trouble, we tend to turn to old friends out of habit or comfort, but this time, it may not work so well. Remember the old Girl Scout song, *Make new friends, but keep the old, one is silver and the other's gold.*

## OLD FRIENDS

I've heard that a widow typically loses 75% of her friends when she loses her husband (I have not learned statistics for men). When I read that statistic, I was somewhat relieved. I had wondered if all our friends just liked Joe better than me, and they had been kindly putting up with me all those years! Elizabeth Bankoff reports that old friends are helpful only during the early stages of grief because married friends felt threatened by a single woman in the group.[16]

After some reflection, I came to understand that it's just natural for friendships to change. Many relationships were built on the couple concept—going out to dinner and concerts as a double date. Many of our friendship couples were also made up by men Joe worked with. So when that work connection ended, so did spontaneous planning of social outings. And when they did kindly think to invite me, there was awkwardness to the situation. I remember the first few times I went out to restaurants with two or three other couples. The table was always set for an even number of people and the unused table setting would glare at me. I was nearly in tears and I'm sure the discomfort paralyzed everyone. It took me awhile to learn to arrive early and just ask the wait staff to adjust the number of settings. I don't arrive early anymore, but I matter-of-factly ask for the adjustment as orders are being made. My point is that our old friends can feel awkward and don't know how to act. It's up to us to make them comfortable, so be specific about what you need.

To maintain old friendships, we need to keep in touch. Remember a birthday or anniversary with a card. Send a clipping from the paper on a topic you know will interest someone. Greet them warmly when you see them in the community. Deliver a meal when you hear they're sick. The idea behind all of this is to keep the lines of communication open. As old friends become more comfortable with you as a single person, and they're not scared to say the wrong thing, they'll start initiating the communication again. Be patient. They're also grieving the loss of a friend and may just feel awkward.

The great thing about old friends is that they share memories with us. I love hearing the anecdotes about Joe that maybe I hadn't heard before. Or they just may be able to laugh with us, remembering antics or a practical joke we all enjoyed together. They also already accept us as we are, with all

---

[16] Bankoff, Elizabeth. Effects of Friendship Support on the Psychological Well-Being of Widows. In Helena Z Lopata and David Maines eds., Friendship in Context. Greenwich, CT: JAI Press, 1990.

our strengths and weaknesses. We can just relax and be ourselves.

**Photo by Emily Steel**

## NEW FRIENDS

Children are taught to share their toys, to say please and thank you, and to invite children to play with them. After the age of five or six, no one teaches us anything about how to make friends. We have to figure it out for ourselves. It's made more difficult by how we live, in separated housing units. And with more and more business and shopping being done on line, even the simple social interactions in the community are less frequent. The sense of a village community is hard to find.

The opportunity to make new friends varies throughout the different ages and stages of life. When our children are young, it's easy to meet other young parents on the playground or at school. But as the only widowed parent in the school, that sets us apart and can make forming new friendships difficult. In addition, caring for children who have lost their mom/dad is excruciatingly difficult and energy consuming. So the time and energy for friends are both very minimal. If we don't have dependent children and are still working, we have a greater opportunity for social activities. We meet more people and are free to go out after work. Then during the retirement years, we need to make the effort to put ourselves in places where people are being sociable. But at no age or stage will people necessarily come to us seeking friendship. We need to decide that friendship is a priority and make the first move.

Though that sounds difficult, the effort is worth it, because the need for new friends is tremendous. We still have a lot of energy and compassion.

We still want to go to the movies and analyze the film immediately afterwards. We don't want to eat alone every night. We may need a ride for a colonoscopy (that's a really good friend!). Sometimes, we want to celebrate some good news or to complain about having had a bad day. We may need a sounding board for brainstorming a problem. We also need to be needed. We like to be asked for advice or to be able to offer consolation. It makes us feel worthwhile.

Socrates advised, "Be slow to fall into friendship; but when thou art in, continue firm and constant. " Making friends takes time because it takes shared experiences to see how compatible you are. Getting into a quick relationship with someone you find that you don't really like being with is much easier than getting out of the relationship. So take your time and avoid long-term commitments until you are comfortable. During this stage, watch for what's important to you. Do they gossip or keep confidences? Do they enjoy doing the same activities that you do? Do they anger easily? Do they seem to live within their budget? Do they have interests or are they always hanging around your house? Do they criticize or look for the good in a person or situation? Do you agree or at least feel tolerance for each other's political or religious views? And, of course, you'll have your own criteria for friends. Think about what kind of people have been great friends for you in the past. If you've made some mistakes choosing friends in the past, this is a great chance for a "do-over."

The best place to start making friends is by finding someone with similar interests. When you're working beside someone on a shared project, you have a ready topic of conversation. Or, if the conversation lags, you have the project to attend. While working together, you'll have a chance to problem solve together, to laugh together, to share stories, and then, maybe to plan another activity together. The activity could be anything—from a maintenance project or a rummage sale at church, to a Habitat for Humanity build, to a hike with the Appalachian Mountain Club, to a pottery or foreign language class. The only important thing is that you enjoy the activity enough to go back often.

The next steps are easier if you're an extrovert, but even introverts can make it through. Both extroverts and introverts make excellent friends. Just be yourself, and as people get to know you, they can't help but love you!

A few hints to get you started:

- Make eye contact, smile, say, "My name is_____" Extend a hand. When they introduce themselves, repeat their name so you can remember it. "It's nice to meet you, John". (Sounds so simple, doesn't it? You can do this!)

- Say, "I'm glad to be here. How can I help?" (Everyone loves someone who is willing to chip in.) If there seems to be a system, ask *how* they want things done. Don't hesitate to ask clarifying questions.

- Ask others how they came to be involved in this activity and why they continue. Ask how newcomers can find a role in the activity.
- If people go out for coffee afterwards, go along. Listen for opportunities for future opportunities to get together.
- When you've made a friendly connection with someone, you can get together outside of the organization where you met, for a meal or even something new that would interest both of you. There may be a presentation at your public library, an outdoor concert, a steam engine exhibit or an air show—anything can be fun!
- Offer to help your new friend with a project they're working on. An extra pair of hands is often helpful.
- Be open and friendly. Keep confidences. Don't gossip. Don't overstay your welcome. Do your fair share of bringing food and cleaning up. Give honest compliments.
- Welcome the next newcomer. Be on the lookout for someone who looks a little lost. Invite them into the activity.

Plan on finding at least a few friends. No one person can replace your late spouse. You'll need someone who likes to talk, someone who will listen, someone who makes you laugh, someone who will give practical advice/help, someone who loves theater, someone who loves travel…. Well, you get the idea. You need several friends.

**Being with your friends helps you validate who you are. When they laugh, you know you're funny. When they share a confidence, you know you're trustworthy. When they ask for advice, you know you are competent. And when you are on the wrong track, good friends will help steer you back. Though peace and happiness begins within, the external support does fuel us and encourages us to be our best selves.**

# *ROMANCE*

*You can't steal second with one foot still on first*

There may come a time when you consider dating again. In the book of Genesis (2:18), the very first book of the Bible, God says, "It is not good that man should be alone". And our wedding vows did include, "until death do us part". So all signs point to it being perfectly permissible and even good, to find a new partner. I believe that we have the capacity to love many people without diminishing the love for any of them. Nevertheless, beginning a new romantic relationship can be both daunting and exhilarating. After all, it's been a long time! So take your time, and just as with any friendship, begin slowly, and get to know one another. Enjoy the journey of the relationship, and allow the feeling to grow naturally. When things go well, your heart swells, you feel energized, and your world expands. Let's consider for a minute whether you're ready to start. It's important to understand your motivation for beginning a romantic relationship. Know what you loved about being married, and know where difficulties in your marriage lay. In other words, know what you need, and know what you are able to give.

There are some bad reasons to start dating. Know that are two people involved in any couple, so it's not right to get involved when the obvious outcome is you will break someone's heart. If there are still pictures of your late spouse on your bedside table, and his/her clothes and toiletries are still where they left them, and if you're still a regular visitor to the cemetery, and if your in-laws still dominate your life, and if all your conversations focus on how sad you are, you are not ready yet to start dating. You might feel lonely, and miss the feel of a person beside you. If you just hate getting into a cold bed, buy a heated mattress pad. And, to be blunt, don't be above some "do it yourself" techniques to meet physical needs. On a gentler note, you may just need physical contact. I was lucky I had my first grandchild soon after my husband died. Being able to hold and rock her was very soothing. Maybe volunteering as a foster grandparent at the hospital would provide some of the snuggling that is so important to every human being.

Men especially are bombarded with casseroles and flirtations from savvy women. Men traditionally have not had the same amount of practice in saying no to women that women have had in saying no to men. An easy way to discourage unwanted attention is to say, "I appreciate your kind and friendly support. But I am still too in love with my spouse to even think about romance with anyone. I respect you too much to lead you on and waste your time." It's honest and it's not hurtful. Men typically remarry within a year of losing their wife. There's no way a year is enough time to recover from the loss, and to assess what you'd like your future to look like. When widowers remarry, half of the marriages end in divorce. Have confidence in your ability to learn to live independently, even if it's difficult at first. Take your time, examine your options, and really know someone before you jump into marriage.

You are ready to start dating again when you feel you have love in your heart that you need to share. You're ready to put someone else's needs on par with your own. You should have cleaned your house of most of the mementos of your marriage. Of course, you can keep enough–the marriage was a big part of your life. But a new person should feel there is room there for them. So be open to celebrating holidays in new ways and going on vacation to new places. And feel really excited about the prospect of going on a date!

Once you start dating, be prepared for a reaction from the people who care about you. Most people will be happy for you. But remember that anytime we make a change, it does affect the people around us. If you have minor children, your concern for them has to come first. Your potential mate needs to understand their emotional needs, and be willing to work with your family to support them. If you have adult children, they will be cautious initially, wanting to protect you from personal hurt or financial harm. Your date should be mature enough to tolerate their scrutiny in an open and loving way. Once the initial check-up is accomplished, adult children should be happy for you and perhaps relieved that someone else is there for you. They should develop a friendly relationship with your date.

Dealing with your in-laws deserves some consideration. If you have minor children, your in-laws may be a big part of your support system. And you are a huge emotional connection to their child. So it's as big a step for them as it is for you. They'll be able to be happy for you, too, if they are made to feel confident they'll still be a big part of their grandchildren's lives. I always say that families are inclusive. We're blessed when more people join the love of our family.

"The right person is more motivation than any widower needs to pack up the past and build a new life," according to *Dating a Widower*[17]. "Our actions set the tone for our children, family, and friends." Accept that he'll always love his first wife, but that you expect to be treated first in his current and future life. Don't settle. "I'm still grieving" is code for I don't love you enough to marry you, but please don't leave me!" Watch how the widower responds to his adult children's juvenile and controlling behaviors. You're an addition, not a replacement.

*The first time someone shows you who they are, believe them.* --Maya Angelou

When I first started dating in the 1960s, I believed that the worst thing that could happen was that I would have a cute little baby and no stable home. Young people today are savvier at preventing unwanted pregnancies, but there is still a long list of things that are dangerous.

The most obvious concern is physical health. HIV rates are growing most quickly in the over-65 age demographic. This is because we thought condoms were just for preventing pregnancy. They're not! They also help prevent transmission of diseases that people don't even know they have. Before embarking on a physical relationship, it's critical you and your partner undergo medical assessment for sexually transmitted diseases. Then, follow the medical advice for treatment and prevention of spreading the disease. This is a societal problem. It should not be considered a character flaw or something to be embarrassed about. You both have the right and

---

[17] Keogh Abel. Dating a Widower: Starting a Relationship with a Man who's Starting Over. Kindle. 2011

responsibility to be honest with one another about this. Know that problems can be managed well, with the correct information.

Before beginning to date, assess yourself in your past relationships. Be alone in a quiet place with a pencil and paper. Write down what went wrong in your past marriage or dating relationship. Try to understand what your role was in the problem. Don't worry about what the other person did or was. You can't change that. In the beginning of the relationship, did you see what you wanted to see, ignoring troubling signals? Did you have respect for the person, or did you look down on them? Did you encourage the person to grow? Were you quick to anger? Were you honest? Did you welcome the people s/he cared about into your life? Were you generous? Were you kind? Were you patient? In order to improve your next relationship, you need to understand what patterns of behavior that you developed during your marriage.

If there is something about your behavior that makes you a risky date, please seek counseling before involving another person with you. Your chance of a successful partnership depends on you entering the relationship as a whole and healthy partner. Also consider, since their death, have you "sanctified" your spouse? If so, it will be difficult for any new person to compete with that partially fictitious memory.

Also know what you want in the relationship. Do you just need a date for a symphony or a wedding? Or do you want a casual friendship, or a friendship with benefits? Or do you want someone to live with you? Do you want marriage? Do you need someone to help you financially? Do you need someone who will help you with minor children? It's fair to the other person to be honest about where you'd like your life to go.

If you are a healthy and safe person, wonderful, but still proceed carefully into the dating scene. Dating puts you in a vulnerable position and you need to have your wits about you. If you choose to start your search online, there are guidelines available from the site you're using. Most will advise you not disclose your personal information, such as full name, phone number, or home address until you have reason to feel confidence. If someone's profile looks too good to be true, trust that intuitive assessment. If someone has many grammatical errors or writes too flirtatiously, let that one go.

When you decide to meet in person, drive yourself to a public place. If you're nervous, ask a friend to sit at a nearby spot to escort you home if necessary. Watch for red flags:

- Does he build himself up and put you down?
- Does she gossip? Does she make disparaging remarks about anyone's appearance, religion, culture?
- Does he give his opinions and not ask yours?

- Is she willing to be open about her past? Does she tend to blame other people for problems?
- Is she willing to give back to the community?
- Does he try to buy you with gifts?
- Is she interested in the people who are important to you?
- Is he excited and supportive of your life dreams?
- Does she have life dreams? Or is she a moocher?
- Is he prudent with the use of alcohol or drugs?
- Who are her friends? Are they engaged in life or are they loafers?
- Is there any evidence of anger management issues?
- Does s/he rush you into the relationship? Do you feel pressured in any way?

Don't hesitate to end that first date with "It was nice to meet you. I wish you all the best, but I don't think we're a good match." If you're asked to expand on the statement and say why, just repeat that you don't think you're a good match. Give a friendly handshake and be on your way. 95% of first encounters end that way. It's so easy to end a relationship before it really begins. If you see one of the red flags, or if there is any cause of discomfort for you, don't hesitate to say good-bye. Sometimes your intuition is the best guide.

# GOAL SETTING

*Start with the end in mind*--Stephen Covey

I've heard goals are just dreams with deadlines. I'm not sure whom to credit for the idea, but I like it. When I was in college, my psychology professor advised us to spend New Year's Day each year writing goals for the year. He suggested that goals be in three categories: personal, professional and financial. Of course, if you have goals outside those areas, include them. This is a tradition my late husband and I continued. Now that I'm widowed, I find that more than ever I need a structure to my time. Without a plan, I find myself wandering, snacking or watching too much television. Having specific and measurable goals gives me purpose.

**Start by reflecting on past successes.** Remember one or more times, planned or unplanned, when something turned out as you'd hoped.

- What qualities or talents did you use?

- What strategies were helpful?

- How did you deal with obstacles?

By recognizing the ingredients of your past success, you start to become aware of your talents. You might realize that you are organized, patient, persistent, a creative problem solver, financially responsible and/ or a good leader. These are qualities you can count on to help with future success. If you're honest, you'll also unveil your weaknesses. It's all right. We all have our weak points. What's important to realize here is we cannot do everything alone. When we recognize a weak point, that's a good time to use the talents of friends or pay people to help.

### Brainstorm Current Goals

Take a few minutes, or even hours, days or weeks, if you like, to daydream, which is far more creative than our teachers gave us credit for. Go for a walk, chop some firewood, or take a bubble bath. Do whatever it takes to get your brain freed up from the everyday clutter. Let your brain wander and conjure. In the quiet, an idea will nudge you. You'll start to feel an energy surging up. It might even feel like joy. Follow the thought. When you are able, write it down or speak into a recorder. During the brainstorming stage, it doesn't need to be practical or make sense. Once you get the hang of this, you'll find that quiet times provide an abundance of creative ideas. In fact, quiet is so rich, you might find yourself seeking it instead of dreading it!

After you've listed several goals, you'll want to choose those you'll pursue with commitment. The end result of achieving the goal should make your life better. **Know why you want to work toward this goal. You should be passionate enough about this, that you'll have the energy to work through difficulties. Knowing how the end result will improve your life will make it more likely you'll follow through**. However, I don't mean to imply the achievement is the only measure of success. I hope the activities involved will also be a positive experience. For example, if you wish to learn to paint, there may not ever be an end to the process. In that goal, there is always a quest for improvement, but the process itself is most rewarding. On the other hand, if it's your goal to organize a closet, there should be the satisfaction of a job well done within a reasonable period of time. It is perfectly acceptable to change a goal once you've started. You may change because a new opportunity has presented itself or because support systems that you counted on are no longer available. Changing a goal does not mean we failed. Sometimes it's smart to be flexible and make necessary adjustments. Just be aware of why you're changing so that you can plan better in the future.

**Before you set your goal in stone,** set yourself up for success by realistically assessing your situation:

- Consider what barriers you anticipate along the way. How will you deal with them?
- Consider possible resources in the community, online or in your own home; what will help support you?
- Consider the time commitment. When can you fit this in?
- Consider the impact on your budget. What other budget item can you modify to allow for this new project?

Big goals are admirable, but can sometimes feel overwhelming. It helps to define short term goals that are small steps toward your long-term goal. An old Chinese proverb states that the longest journey begins with a single step. The small steps you make toward your goal encourage you to keep going. Short-term goals ought to be well defined and have an estimated date of completion, so that you know when you have achieved it. For example, if your goal is to organize a closet, your short term goals might include separating the contents into keep, sell, donate and throw away piles; then follow through on each required action. The time frame here might be three days. Your second short term goal would be to determine and buy the appropriate types of storage containers. One day should be enough for this step. The final short-term goal would be to organize the desired stuff in such a way that you can find it when you want it. Again, one day should be enough for the final step. By breaking it down, the task is more manageable. The same strategy works for bigger goals. My friend, Lee Toth, decided to learn Spanish. Her short-term objectives were to take Spanish lessons, to read Spanish literature in a book group, to travel to South America to volunteer as a nurse, and then to hike Machu Pichu. After five years, she has now met her goal and can converse and read easily in Spanish. Along the way, she was open to opportunities that she hadn't considered when she developed her goals. She learned to appreciate South American art, to dance the tango and to cook. These were natural progressions along her path of learning Spanish. Though she diverged a bit, the new opportunities actually enriched her growth. So feel free to modify goals as you progress. If you change or defer a short-term goals, always know why and make a conscious decision to digress.

Some people are disciplined enough to work independently and stay focused. Many of us benefit from camaraderie along the way. The benefit of accountability is demonstrated by the success of such organizations as Weight Watchers. If there is a club or organization that matches your goal, consider joining. A good organization keeps you on task and provides educational resources. An added bonus is that you'll meet people with similar interests, creating an opportunity for potential friendships. You may also learn from their experiences or share resources.

If there's not an established group, you can partner with a "goal buddy." Talk about what you need from a goal buddy. Maybe it's a sounding board for ideas or a deadline for meeting short term goals. And know, too, what you are willing and able to give as a goal buddy. The two of you could be working on totally different goals, but still be very supportive of each other. The two of you would meet on a schedule that you decide. You'd help each other set goals, write plans and encourage each other. Don't forget to celebrate meeting short-term and final goals! Also important is showing appreciation to those who support you along the way. Though our goals are important, equally important are the relationships that we build.

## *PERSONAL GOAL*
**Long Term Goal**


Rationale: It will make my life (or my favorite charity) better by


**Short term goal #1**


Resources needed:


Completed by date:

**Short term goal #2**


Resources needed:


Completed by date:

**Short term goal #3**


Resources needed:


Completed by date:

**Long term goal will be met by**:

Success measured by:

Success will be celebrated by:

# *PROFESSIONAL GOAL*

**Long Term Goal**


Rationale: It will make my life (or my favorite charity) better by


**Short term goal #1**


Resources needed:


Completed by date:

**Short term goal #2**


Resources needed:


Completed by date:

**Short term goal #3**


Resources needed:


Completed by date:

**Long term goal will be met by**:

Success measured by:

Success will be celebrated by:

# *FINANCIAL GOAL*

**Long Term Goal**


Rationale: It will make my life (or my favorite charity) better by


**Short term goal #1**


Resources needed:


Completed by date:

**Short term goal #2**


Resources needed:


Completed by date:

**Short term goal #3**


Resources needed:


Completed by date:

**Long term goal will be met by**:

Success measured by:

Success will be celebrated by::

# USING CONSULTANTS

Because I like feeling competent and independent, I try to do a good deal of my own work. It also saves money to do-it-yourself. But there are times when I do need to call in people who are more skilled than I am. It's a good idea to develop a team of people before an emergency develops. My singles group at church developed a list of reliable specialists that we share among ourselves, and we continually add to the list. Word of mouth referrals help ensure the honesty and competence of those we hire.

The personal recommendation is especially important when someone will do work inside your home. Be sure that the person is licensed and bonded. They need to carry liability insurance. They need to report income and pay their own taxes.

When you find someone reliable and competent, show your appreciation by paying your bill on time. And if you refer your friends, you'll find yourself to be a very popular customer, getting prompt attention when you need it!

Be careful of people who knock on your door or phone you to offer to do work for you. Be sure to get references. There was one man who knocked on a widow's door, saying that her late husband gave his word that he should cut down a tree in her yard. Though she didn't know anything about it, she wanted to honor her husband's commitment. Later, she learned that he did the same thing to another widow.

**Develop your own list of specialists, so that when you have a problem, you're halfway to a solution.**

## *Important People*

| | |
|---|---|
| Yard work | |
| Snow plow | |
| Plumber | |
| Carpenter | |
| Handyman | |
| Auto repair | |
| Electrician | |
| Locksmith | |
| Insurance salesperson | |
| Attorney | |
| Accountant | |
| Dentist, oral surgeon, periodontist | |
| Psychologist, social worker, counselor | |
| Primary care physician | |
| Real estate agent | |
| Banker | |
| Financial advisor | |
| Housecleaners | |
| Taxis and other agencies that offer transportation | |
| Home health aides and companions | |
| Neighbors | |
| Computer expert | |
| Seamstress or tailor | |
| Caterer | |
| House cleaner | |
| Pet sitter | |
| Vet | |
| Dog walker | |
| Babysitter | |
| | |
| | |
| | |

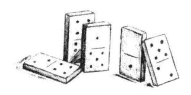

# GETTING OUR AFFAIRS IN ORDER

We've been through enough after the loss of our spouse to understand how difficult it is for those left behind. The least we can do is to have the business aspect of the loss be as easy as possible for those we'll leave behind. And we certainly want to minimize conflict among our loved ones. So being clear is very important. I organize a full-day retreat at my church every other year called, *Gifts and Grace in Life's Final Days*. Presentations are made by attorneys, life insurance agents, proponents of planned giving, judge of probate, funeral home directors, hospice and the pastor. Participants are given a workbook that is published by the United Church of Christ. Similar books may be available from your financial advisor. Though specifics will vary from state to state, there are certain commonalities to consider.

**In your file cabinet, you should have:**
o   Last Will and Testament
o   Medical power of attorney
o   Power of attorney
o   Living will with end of life directives (your doctor should have a copy of this)
o   A copy of your spouse's will
o   Your spouse's birth and death certificates
o   Your marriage certificate
o   You and your spouse's social security numbers
o   Tax returns for the past 5 years
o   Your most recent W-2 forms or federal self-employment tax return

o Financial information, including savings/checking accounts, retirement funds, brokerage accounts, retirement plans, stock options, trust documents. Include IOUs for loans you have made. Include account numbers, passwords. Be sure beneficiary information is up to date on your retirement funds and brokerage accounts

o Key to safe deposit box

o Insurance policies (life, homeowners, car). All of your insurance policies should have the correct beneficiaries listed

o Real estate: deeds, mortgage statements, leases, deed to car.

o Debts: credit cards, loans.

o Documentation of burial plot or funeral arrangements.

Note—This list is not intended to be legal counsel or to replace a consultation with an attorney in your state.

**Plan your funeral and service.** If you choose, you may prepay your funeral and make all the arrangements, including readings and hymns that are meaningful to you. When you prepay for a funeral, the money goes into a general fund. So no matter where you live now and where you are when you need it, the fund will cover the expenses at any funeral home. You may also purchase your cemetery or cremation plot in advance.

**Leave a clear record of your assets**. Include the names of financial institutions, the account numbers and contact information. If you manage assets on line, your executor should have access to your passwords. Be sure that your executor knows how to access all of your important paperwork. If you have a financial advisor, his or her contact information should be available. It's a good idea for your executor to have copies of all the legal papers.

**You'd be very kind to do some housecleaning**, getting rid of things you no longer need or want. It's a chance to give special items personally to people and to tell them the story that makes the item special. For things in useable condition, consider charitable donations. Some agencies, like Big Brother Big Sister, will come and pick up your things. Tools and items that could be used for home improvement can be given to Habitat for Humanity. Clearing out your space of things you'll never use will be a help to your children and will provide you with the space you now need for your new hobbies.

Some of us have difficulty talking about important issues with our children. In some cases, it might be wise to keep financial information close. For example, if a child or his/her spouse is an addict or a no-good moocher, we might not be so willing to open our records. But if your kids are self-sufficient and mature, then it's very smart to open the books. They might be more current and savvy with finance. We don't need to follow their advice, but we'd be smart to at least listen.

Adult children generally have our best interest at heart. They are the ones most likely to make decisions for us if we are incapacitated. **We need to be very clear about what we want if we can no longer take care of ourselves.** I've already talked about having long-term care insurance. A Living Will helps when we're actually dying, but how we want to live when we cannot take care of ourselves is something we must communicate. I took my mother-in-law, and 20 years later, my mother, on tours of local long-term care facilities. Some were pure nursing homes and others were places for transitional living, from independent cottages to assisted living, to a nursing home setting. We made these tours while they were in their 80's but still in good health. My mother-in-law had been a nurse and asked great questions. She actually chose the nursing home where she ended up living for 10 years. Because it was her choice, she accepted it as well as anyone could. And it certainly reduced my guilt about not being able to care for her at home any longer. My mother has made her selection and is happily looking forward to new friends and an active recreation schedule. A nice aspect to this is that it is her choice. I have six siblings and the discussion around "Mom would have wanted" could have been quite tangled. I have done enough care giving around my mother-in-law and my late husband, that I realize that it is difficult. I've told my children that they don't have to take care of me, but they need to be sure someone will. I also told them that I trust their judgment, and if there comes a time that I cannot make good decisions that they should do what they think is best for me. Even if I develop dementia, and protest against having help, I now in my right mind give them permission to do what is right. Meanwhile, I try to live a healthy lifestyle so it will be a long time before they have to worry about me.

A strategy to help ensure that your wishes for living with assistance are implemented is to register with a skilled nursing facility of your choice. It can take time and effort to register with a long-term care facility. In my state of Connecticut, when a person is discharged from the hospital, but is not able to live independently at home, s/he can be discharged to any skilled nursing facility within 50 miles. You may have no choice in where you are sent. But if you have been pre-registered with the facility of your choice, you will be sent there. In the event that the chosen facility does not have a bed available, you will be first in line for the next available bed. So once you select the facility that you want, ask about how to pre-register.

Though it may seem a bit morbid, completing these steps while you're feeling healthy isn't taxing. Moreover, the process could unearth some unsettled issues, and this will be your opportunity to clear them up. Once done, you'll feel a comfort of being organized and settled.

# TRAVEL

Once your affairs are in order, feel free to take a vacation! Vacations are not a luxury, but necessary for the purpose of recharging your batteries. Rest is integral to seeing things in perspective and to thinking creatively. Every faith tradition observes Sabbath. It is not a suggestion to rest on the Sabbath; it's a commandment. Since the beginning of time, the value of rest has been honored. I know there are all sorts of arguments against going on vacation–"there isn't enough money," "people here depend on me," "I don't want to travel by myself." It's important to schedule time away from the stress and responsibilities of everyday life so you can return refreshed, renewed and better equipped to manage your life well. Surely, you deserve it after all that responsible behavior! **Treat yourself as you would treat a good friend. Allow some easing of the load, some good rest and even some fun!**

As much as I love my home, I also love the adventure of travel. I think that we all need a respite from our daily routine and stresses. Travel makes all things possible, and so decision making is a real art. It makes sense to me that vacations should be very different from what we do every day. If our days are full and hectic and stressed, then vacation should provide rest, rejuvenate our creativity and lower our blood pressure. If our days are routine and easy, then we can seek more challenges in our vacation.

The easiest vacations are done right from your home; this is a "stay-cation". Plan a week of day outings well in advance. Just as if you were out of town, refrain from household chores and worry. Avoid phone calls unless they're from fun people. Maybe even hire someone to clean your house while you are out one day. Eat out as much as possible. Your planning will guide you to museums, theaters, shops and historical sites. Other days, you can hike in state parks or do other active things, like kayaking or snow shoeing. Get tickets to a ball game; see if the stadium offers tours. Visit a nice library in the region, peruse magazines. Perhaps try an art class or a cooking class. End the week with a spa day, getting a massage or manicure. If you find a museum that you like, join. They'll send you information throughout the year about special events. It might grow into a volunteer activity. Arrange to connect with friends on some of the outings. This sort of vacation is very satisfying and quite affordable. Once you've done this in your own geographic area, you'll realize that the same strategy could be implemented anywhere. Have some fun selecting a city or resort area, then make a hotel reservation and plan an overnight trip there.

I'm sure you know about guided bus tours that are available almost everywhere. Senior centers and local symphonies offer great outings. They're popular because they are convenient, reliable and affordable. Certainly try more than one, as there are some differences in the amenities provided. Some provide a guide, tickets to shows, hotel accommodations. Others are simply transportation.

Road Scholars, (www.roadscholar.org), previously known as Elderhostel, offers a HUGE variety of options for people of all ages. These vacations go all over the world, with the goal of learning about something in the company of other learners. You'll have access to guides who are knowledgeable and generous. I highly recommend you get their catalog. It'll get you realizing how easy it is to have a very exciting vacation. One of my neighbors took her two teen-aged grandchildren to Paris through the Road Scholars. The young people spent the day with a Parisian high school history teacher while the adults toured the city. When they met for dinner, they had so much enthusiasm to share. They found they had enough time together, but also discovered there was time for age appropriate activities for all.

There are other learning centered vacations. The John C Campbell Folk Art School in North Carolina (www.folkschool.org) offers a myriad of week-end and week-long classes in such things as woodworking, blacksmithing, woodcarving, fine arts, banjo and textile arts. You'll live with several others in a house on the property, and share healthy and delicious meals in a dining hall with about 120 fellow campers. Evenings offer folk music and dancing. Mystic Seaport in Connecticut (http://www.mysticseaport.org) offers boatbuilding courses. Kirpula in Massachusetts offers yoga retreats. There are bridge conventions and stamp collecting conventions. The nice thing about all of these is that it's easy to attend alone. You're put together with people of like interests. Your housing is taken care of. You have people to eat with.

There are active vacations too. You can hike through Zion and Bryce Canyons with guides from REI (www.rei.com/adventures). You can Google bicycle tours of every state and country. Maybe consider a dude ranch?

You could also spend a week working on a political campaign, or join in a political march. Or stay home and write letters to your elected officials to support a cause you believe in.

There are religious retreats. Often these are for a weekend and center on a certain topic. There is generally some group time where a leader presents information, followed by some discussion or activity to explore the ideas presented. It was on such a retreat that I learned about labyrinth meditation. Another retreat I attended focused on dream analysis. Such retreats also leave time for meditation, taking walks outdoors and good meals. They tend to be very affordable. There are retreats especially for people who have experienced a loss. See CampWidow.org or WidowedPathfinder.com for more specifics.

One of my favorite types of vacation is a volunteer vacation. These can be found through your house of worship or online. Clubs like the Appalachian Mountain Club seek volunteers for trail maintenance. There is also a book, *The 100 Best Volunteer Vacations*.[18] Going on a volunteer vacation provides the company of other volunteers, who tend to be really great people. It also affords the opportunity to live among the locals, who are welcoming and appreciative of your efforts. You may just need to pay for your travel to the destination. Sometimes, a nominal fee is requested for housing and meals. My niece, Anne Murphy, who is an attorney, scheduled a volunteer vacation to Kathmandu, Napal, that coincided with the first anniversary of my husband's death. I decided to join her to distract me from the date. I also believe that the best way to mental health is to care about others. We stayed in a concrete house with 10 volunteers from around the world, and we spent our days serving the Nepal Orphan's Home. The home was well run, with lots of love and positive activities for the kids. But the children were in school most of the day, so we sought other work. Being a physical therapist, I wanted to find the orphans with special needs. For that, we travelled to the public orphanage. We identified a few children whom I thought we could help in just 3 months. One four year old boy learned to walk and has been adopted. One girl who was deaf received proper medical treatment and now can talk and sing. It's a long story, but we have continued to care for the children. Anne set up a non-profit organization. We now have 10 children who are visually impaired. If you want to know more, check our website at ***aakritiskids.org***.

---

[18] National Geographic 2009

If you have any talent or skill, there's a volunteer vacation that's right for you. Most organizations consider a warm heart to be a welcome talent. There are many near your home as well as around the world. You'll come home with greater appreciation for what you have and a sense of accomplishment for making the world just a little better. And you'll probably make friends with some great people.

There are luxury vacations, and sometimes that's just what's needed. I find a little luxury goes a long way, so these vacations for me are usually just one overnight in a nearby city at a fancy hotel. I take advantage of every amenity, from the pool to the chocolate on the pillow. My most recent such trip was to the Ritz Carlton on the Battery in New York City. The room had a telescope that was pointed at the Statue of Liberty. Of all our national landmarks, that one is my favorite. I felt great joy looking at it, and appreciating the hardships my grandparents endured when they emigrated here so I could have a better life. A luxury vacation gives us time to appreciate all the blessings that we do have. If you can't afford an overnight in such a place, dressing up and going there for tea will give you the same feeling of opulence.

At the end of vacation, we should feel refreshed and infused with energy. We shouldn't be five pounds heavier or in debt up to our ears. That just piles the stress back on. Rather than increased debt or waist size, we should have the joy of photographs taken to help remember our adventure. Try to keep in touch if you made a friend along the way. And start planning that next trip!

# MISTAKES

Remember that trying and failing is a combined strategy of experiential learning. There are other less painful ways to learn. If possible, it's always better to learn from someone else's mistakes than from your own. This book is full of information and stories that will help you to learn from others' experiences. But even when you've made well informed decisions, things don't always turn out as you've hoped. When that happens, don't be too hard on yourself. Try to analyze why you made the choice that you did. Being intentional about decision making allows us to make better decisions in the future. It's good to be aware so that you don't keep making the same mistake. Take some time to reflect, brush yourself off, and be very kind to yourself. You'll have another chance, and you just might get it right next time.

# CONCLUSION

Here's one thing for sure—we've each lost a spouse or a partner. That could be where our commonality ends. Perhaps you're younger, I'm older and we're different races. Maybe one of us is rich, the other poor and we come from different faith backgrounds. Maybe one of us had great marriage; maybe not—we could be relieved that it's over. You could have a wonderful family that supports you, while I support my family. Despite these differences, whatever they may be—we have a kinship, a common understanding only those who've lost a spouse can share. And now more than ever, having friends we know, trust and like is so important to our physical and emotional health and happiness. And the secret to lasting, flourishing friendship? To be present and to care.

Remember, true friendship and many other gifts explored in this book—like financial health, desirable work and hobbies, and a satisfying faith practice—are within your grasp, when you stay open to opportunities and focus on what's important to you. Creating your own transformational vision of how you wish to live your life is the key. It takes reflection, organization and action, but you can do it! Armed with your vision, this book and the lessons it teaches, you can shed the needless worries surrounding the unknowns in your life, and begin to fly once again, maybe even higher than ever before. So treasure this stage of widow/er-hood. It's your opportunity to savor personal growth, creativity, and to become your best, most aware, loving and generous self yet.

## I Wish for You

A good night's sleep
Under a safe roof,
The sound of birds outside your window
A good cup of coffee
Books, music, art
Work that engages your intellect and talents
Play that captivates
A hug from a friend
Heart hinges that swing wide open
Peace among those you love
Memories of days gone by
Joyful anticipation of the days ahead.

# A NOTE FROM THE AUTHOR

I consider marriage to be Act I of our lives. This marriage, which began with vows to "love until death do us part", was the core of our life. It gave structure to our home, to our family, and to our relationships in the community. When a spouse dies, the very foundation upon which we built our lives is shaken.

The ensuing time is one of intermission. This is a dark time, filled with a wide range of emotions. It may be shock when the death was unexpected. For others, after a prolonged illness, there may be some relief. For some, there might be anger, or guilt, or disappointment that dreams went unfulfilled. There may be anxiety about how to function independently. For most, there's sadness. There is sadness that hopes and dreams won't come true, and there is sadness for what has been lost. Each person grieves in a unique way, based on the quality and style of the relationship with their spouse, and based on their personality and culture. For those who are grieving, there are support groups available in local communities.

But there comes a time in the grieving process, the "intermission", when we perceive a light flickering in the darkness. We start to perceive a spring in our step again, and our energy level starts to return to normal. When you see that light flicker, you know it's time to go back in for Act II. The problem is, we never planned for an Act II. In other aspects of our lives, such as parenting or career choice, we had years of joyful planning and the mentorship of so many. But there has been no joyful anticipation for this stage of life. We've done little to prepare ourselves for this major life change. In many ways, the loneliness of this stage compounds the problems. But you are not alone. There are 5 million Americans widowed every year. This book is a way to strategize how to live well despite disappointment.

This book is about Act II, which honors and remembers the marriage, and many themes will continue. And in some way, we honor the memory of our late spouse. But *After the Loss of a Spouse: What's Next? o* will also help readers explore the questions about life ahead.

Joanne Moore can be reached at jmoore@widowedpathfinder.com.